TAROT
BY NUMBERS

Inspiring | Educating | Creating | Entertaining

© 2022 Quarto Publishing Group USA Inc.
Text © 2022 Elizabeth Dean

First Published in 2022 by Fair Winds Press, an imprint of The Quarto Group,
100 Cummings Center, Suite 265-D, Beverly, MA 01915, USA.
T (978) 282-9590 F (978) 283-2742 Quarto.com

Fair Winds Press titles are also available at discount for retail, wholesale, promotional, and bulk purchase. For details, contact the Special Sales Manager by email at specialsales@quarto.com or by mail at The Quarto Group, Attn: Special Sales Manager, 100 Cummings Center, Suite 265-D, Beverly, MA 01915, USA.

26 25 24 23 22   1 2 3 4 5

ISBN: 978-0-7603-7526-6

Digital edition published in 2022
eISBN: 978-0-7603-7527-3

Library of Congress Cataloging-in-Publication Data available.

Cover design and page layout: Landers Miller Design

Illustrations from the Rider-Waite Tarot Deck® reproduced by permission of U.S. Game Systems, Inc., Stamford, CT 06902 USA. Copyright © 1971 by U.S. Games Systems, Inc. Further reproduction prohibited. The Rider-Waite Tarot Deck® is a registered trademark of U.S. Games Systems, Inc.

Page 52: Source gallica.bnf.fr / BnF

Printed in China

TAROT BY NUMBERS

LEARN THE CODES
THAT UNLOCK
THE MEANING OF
THE CARDS

✴ LIZ DEAN ✴

FAIR WINDS

CONTENTS

INTRODUCTION:

WHAT'S IN A TAROT NUMBER?

6

1

THE MAJOR ARCANA

CARDS BY NUMBERS

17

2

THE MINOR ARCANA

CARDS BY NUMBERS

44

3

TIMING TECHNIQUES

AND INTUITION

85

4

NUMBER TECHNIQUES

IN TAROT SPREADS

107

5

YOUR BIRTH CARDS

AND TAROTSCOPE

141

INTRODUCTION:
WHAT'S IN A TAROT NUMBER?

The numbers on your tarot cards are an essential tool for navigating your deck, but they also hold symbolic potential, just like any other image on the cards. And as symbols rather than quantities, they take us to the realm of imagination and intuition: the soulful place from which we divine.

Whether you're a beginner or a tarot afficionado, *Tarot by Numbers* offers you a truly accessible way to make meaning from the cards before you. Here, you are invited not only to discover the symbolic meaning of numbers but also to apply this knowledge to your card interpretations for insightful and rewarding readings.

Use this book to:

- ✳ Understand the symbolic meanings of the numbers on your cards

- ✳ Choose a spread with a particular number of cards to reflect your question

- ✳ Discover the numerological links between groups of cards

- ✳ Learn timing spreads and techniques, plus give intuition-based timings

- ✳ Find your tarot birth cards and see your yearly cards in your tarotscope

What's in the Deck?

The traditional tarot deck comprises seventy-eight cards. Of these, twenty-two are known as the major arcana (or trumps or keys), and the remaining fifty-six are known as the minor arcana. The word *arcana* means "secret." The major arcana talks to us of life changes and far-reaching decisions and experiences, and the minor arcana deals with life's day-to-day issues. The minor arcana cards fall into four suits: Cups, Swords, Pentacles, and Wands. There are fourteen cards in each suit, with Ace through Ten and a Page, Knight, Queen, and King. Some decks may have different names for their suits and/or extra cards, but most follow the traditional deck structure.

Interpreting 78

The number 78 itself can be seen as significant: 7 is the number of potential and 8 signifies change, reward, and renewal (see page 11). This is what tarot can offer us—a way to realize our potential for positive change. And this is the approach in *Tarot by Numbers*: to work with numbers to divine meaning.

Throughout, this book is illustrated with the Rider Waite Smith tarot, or RWS. First published in England in 1909, it is the most significant deck of the twentieth century and has become the template for the majority of tarots since. Its name derives from Rider, the publisher; A. E. Waite, the creator; and Pamela Colman Smith, the illustrator. Colman Smith and Waite were both members of the Hermetic Order of the Golden Dawn, a secret society dedicated to occult wisdom and spiritual development. The RWS deck is a pictorial language that many tarot readers share.

A CURIOUS CALCULATION

Sir Cyril Pearson (1866–1921), writing under the pseudonym Professor P. R. S. Foli, published what he termed "a curious calculation" for playing cards in his 1915 book *Fortune Telling by Cards*. By adding up the quantity of cards and suit symbols, and by giving each Court card the number value of 10, he arrived at 365, the number of days in a year. We can take a similar approach with tarot—and if you are a beginner, this may help you recall the structure of the deck.

Add the numbers on the major arcana cards:
0 + 1 + 2 + 3 + and so on, up to card 21.

Total of major arcana numbers:
231
Number of minor arcana cards:
56
Number of cards in the deck:
78

Total:
365

Numbering Origins

The oldest Italian tarot cards, which date from the fifteenth century, were unnumbered, and were used for gaming rather than fortune-telling. Tarot scholar Michael Dummett theorizes that a player had to know the order of trumps (major arcana cards) by heart, and that the order varied depending on the city. As the game of tarot became popular throughout Italy, more decks evolved. Some had fewer or more than seventy-eight cards; the minchiate, for example, had ninety-seven cards. Numbering was introduced to solve the problem of recall.

During the sixteenth century, tarot cards spread beyond Italy. The earliest known deck to contain numbered tarot cards is the 1557 Catelin Geofroy tarot, printed in Lyon, France, which has Strength as card XI and Justice as VIII. The Marseilles tarots, produced in the Marseilles area from the seventeenth century, maintained this order, and it was not until the Rider Waite Smith deck of 1909 that Justice became XI and Strength VIII. The deck's creator, A. E. Waite, made the swap so the cards' symbols of the lion (Leo) and the scales (Libra) aligned with their zodiac signs (see page 98). This is the standard sequence of the majority of tarot decks today.

Arabic and Roman Numbers in Tarot

The number form we use today—0, 1, 2, 3, 4, 5, 6, 7, 8, 9 and beyond—are known as Arabic numerals. Created by mathematicians in India between the sixth and seventh centuries, the system was developed by Arabic and Persian mathematicians and around the twelfth century introduced into Europe.

Roman numerals, which had no glyph for zero, date back to the eighth to ninth century BCE. This system was based on ancient Etruscan numerals, which had been adapted from Greek Attic symbols. Roman numerals were in common use until the fourteenth century, before the advent of the Indo-Arabic system, although they are still used today in certain circumstances—clockfaces, book chapters, the copyright date for movies and television programs, and of course, tarot.

The Rider Waite Smith tarot uses Roman numerals throughout. Other tarots use this convention or have a mixture of Roman and Arabic numerals; some are all Arabic numbers. If you're unfamiliar with Roman numerals, the list below is your guide to the numbers on your cards.

ROMAN	ARABIC	ROMAN	ARABIC	ROMAN	ARABIC
I	1	VIII	8	XV	15
II	2	IX	9	XVI	16
III	3	X	10	XVII	17
IV	4	XI	11	XVIII	18
V	5	XII	12	XIX	19
VI	6	XIII	13	XX	20
VII	7	XIV	14	XXI	21

In Roman numerals, I = 1. V = 5. X = 10. When a digit appears before a V or X, it means V or X minus that number. So IX is 10 − 1 = 9. When a digit comes after a V or X, it means V or X plus that number. Therefore, XVIII is 10 + 5 + 3 = 18.

Number as Idea

Numerology, the study of the metaphysical meaning of numbers, is found in ancient practices and philosophical systems from Pythagoras and the I Ching to Kabbalah and Chaldean numerology. In tarot, number interpretations evolved from the Pythagorean system and the Tree of Life, the diagram of creation that is a central tenet of Kabbalah (see page 157).

Greek mathematician and philosopher Pythagoras of Samos (570–490 BCE) perceived the universe as a series of mathematical relationships and considered numbers to have sacred meanings. Numbers 1 through 10 told the story of spiritual evolution, from 1 as a symbol for God or source to 10 as a symbol for perfection and completion. Pythagoras's number interpretations are the basis of contemporary numerology, which interprets nine rather than ten numbers as personality types.

Contemporary Pythagorean Number Associations

NUMBER		PLANETS	ASSOCIATIONS
1	Monad	Sun	Divine intelligence, unity, oneness
2	Dyad	Moon	Duality, opposition, integration
3	Triad	Jupiter	Achievement, intelligence
4	Tetrad	Uranus	Establishment, stability
5	Pentad	Mercury	Experience
6	Hexad	Venus	Harmony, perfection
7	Heptad	Neptune	Mysteries, discernment
8	Ogdoad	Saturn	Enterprise, transformation, renewal
9	Ennead	Mars	Courage, intensity, higher wisdom

In the ancient Pythagorean system, 10 was seen as the sacred number of the universe, meaning perfection and completion. Number 5 meant marriage (in tarot, 5 or V is the number of the Hierophant or priest, conductor of weddings). The meaning derives from the "wedding," or sum, of numbers 2 and 3. The number 2 was considered a female number, and 3 a male number. In the Pythagorean system, even numbers were female and odd numbers male, apart from the number 1, which had no set gender. It becomes gendered when it is added to itself—so 1 + 1 = 2, female, while 1 + 1 + 1 = 3, male.

Before the discovery of Neptune (1846) and Uranus (1930), numbers 4 and 7 were associated as follows:

＊ **Number 4** was aligned with the Earth or setting Sun rather than Uranus, and it also took the meaning of Justice.

＊ **Number 7** was aligned with the full Moon rather than Neptune, with the meaning of magic, intuition, and wisdom.

Basic Techniques

If you're a seasoned tarot reader, skip ahead. If not, welcome! Here's how to ask a question, shuffle your cards, and choose cards for a reading. You will need:

✴ A tarot deck of your choice. Work with a deck that calls to you and with which you feel a connection. This may not be the deck you admire the most; some decks may be exquisitely beautiful but do not "flow" for you during a reading. This kind of deck may be perfect for a one-card meditation rather than a tarot reading.

✴ A bag or wrap with which to store and protect your cards when they are not in use. Tarot bags come in many colors. Some tarot readers prefer black, the color of protection; purple, for intuition; or blue, for truth and communication.

✴ A cloth on which to lay out your cards for a reading. This can be any square of fabric, purchased or homemade. Choose a color and texture that feel right to you.

THE FOOL

STRENGTH

THE WORLD

Attuning to a New Deck

Hold your cards to your heart. Close your eyes and begin to sense your energy passing into the cards as the symbols on the cards awaken to you. Do this for a few minutes every day for the first week. Handle the cards often, familiarizing yourself with the numbers and images. Don't let others casually pick up your deck; your cards carry your energy imprint and are just for you.

A traditional way to attune to a new deck is to sleep with it under your pillow for seven days.

Cleansing Your Deck: Knock Once

Before you begin a tarot reading, clear the deck of any residual energy by spreading your cards into a fan shape and then blowing over them. Then gather them back into a pile and knock once on the top. Alternatively, use the counting by heart technique (see page 14).

Shuffling and Making a Request

Before you shuffle your cards, take a breath. Center yourself and think about what you'd like to explore. Formulate an open request that allows all possibilities, such as, "Show me what I need to see about my life now," or "Please tell me about [this situation]."

If you ask a specific question with a yes/no answer, you limit your expectations of the reading and potentially block other information from coming through. For example, a closed question, such as, "Will he come back?" begs a yes or no, which we immediately begin to search for in the cards. We might overlook some cards in the spread that don't seem to address the question. If reading for someone else, we come under pressure to deliver a definitive answer, which is not the purpose of a tarot reading at all. The person you read for makes their own decisions and creates their own future; the cards act as mirrors and guides along the way.

When you have settled on your request, shuffle it into the cards. This just means to think of your request while you're shuffling. Shuffling helps you get into a tarot mindset, because it gives your hands and left brain a task. While your conscious, logical self is occupied, your creative right brain, the seat of your intuition, can come to the fore to help you read your cards. You'll know you are in your right brain—or "right mind"—when you feel more relaxed, calm, and ready to read.

COUNTING BY HEART

Counting by heart is counting out your cards to the rhythm of your heartbeat. You can do this before you shuffle to clear any residual energy attached to the cards. If you've been using your cards a lot, this technique releases the accumulated energy of past readings. And if you haven't read your cards for a while, it helps you reconnect with them; you can refamiliarize yourself with every card in just a minute or two.

Place your hand over your heart or feel your pulse.
Feel the rhythm of your heartbeat and count the beats until you feel a regular pace . . . 1, 2, 3, 4. Say the numbers aloud.
To the beat of your heart, place a card from your deck to the left and then a card to the right. Repeat until you have two piles of faceup cards. Shuffle your cards.

Syncing your card count with your heartbeat helps you clear down the deck and brings you into a heart-centered space for a reading.

Choosing Cards for a Tarot Spread

After shuffling, you're ready place your cards in a layout, or spread.
There are three basic ways to do this:

* Hold the deck facedown. With your left hand—traditionally the
  "hand of fate"—take out the cards you need, one by one. This is
  perfect for readings with just a few cards.

* Place the cards facedown in a fan shape and choose your cards
  with your left hand.

* Cut the deck twice so you have three piles of cards. Choose a pile,
  gather the other two piles under it, and deal the cards from the top.

If you are reading for another person, use the three piles method and
ask them to choose the pile. If you are reading online, ask them to visualize
three piles of cards before them and select one—their left, the center, or
their right, which translates as your right, the center, or your left.

Spreads and Significators

Place your cards in the order shown in your chosen spread. They will usually
be facedown, unless the spread uses a Significator. A Significator card
represents you or the person you are reading for. It is chosen after shuffling
and is placed faceup. A Significator card can also represent the overall theme
of a reading.

To turn over your facedown cards, flip them sideways rather than top to
bottom. If you turn them top to bottom, you will reverse cards that should
be read faceup, and vice versa. Upright cards take on a different meaning
when reversed.

Reversals

Every card in the deck has an upright meaning and a reversed meaning.
A reversed card is upside down and, with few exceptions, tends to have a
cautionary or negative meaning. Reversals occur during shuffling; you may
begin with all upright cards, but some may randomly invert. Many tarotists
today do not use reversals in their readings, and if a reversed card appears
in a spread, they simply turn it upright. This is because, having studied tarot,
they bring the meanings of both upright and reversed positions into the
reading and intuit the most relevant interpretation.

1

THE MAJOR ARCANA CARDS BY NUMBERS

●

The twenty-two cards of the major arcana present a journey of life, death, and rebirth. The numbers on the cards reveal the stages of this journey, which is known either as the Fool's Journey, after card 0, the Fool, or the Hero's Journey.

THE HERO'S JOURNEY AND THE FOOL

The Hero's Journey is an archetypal story structure you'll instantly recognize. A young hero on a quest finds themselves in a supernatural wilderness; they locate their treasure, but it is guarded by a monster. To vanquish the monster, the hero must enter a place of darkness and fight for the prize. Through this challenge, they discover their true nature or identity. They return to the familiar world with new wisdom and powers, forever changed by the experience. This is a highly simplified version, but this narrative and its variations are the core of many of our myths, fairy tales, and stories, from Theseus killing the minotaur to Luke Skywalker battling Darth Vader.

The Hero's Journey is the journey of the tarot's Fool, a young person on the cusp of adult life about to risk an adventure. Along the way, they must confront not only the outer world but also their inner demons if they are to realize their true spiritual nature and know their destiny. When their soul's lessons are complete, they return to the world reborn. The Fool's number, 0, is the cosmic egg of potential. Zero is also the shape of the mandorla wreath on card XXI The World. In this way, the Fool's 0 signifies a never-ending cycle that is the eternal nature of the soul.

In Jungian psychology, the Fool or Hero's Journey charts the soul's journey toward individuation. Individuation is the process of increased self-awareness. By becoming more self-aware, we can learn to recognize and heal the tension between our conscious and unconscious selves. This brings the experience of wholeness, as all parts of the self become integrated. We see this integration on card XXI The World, where male and female are combined in one figure, which represents the joyful soul of the world. In this way, individuation, also known as *self-actualization*, is ideal personal growth. Growth is also symbolized by the number 3 for III The Empress (the sum of the digits of the World's number, 21; see page 37). Many people see the tarot as a psychological tool, helping them heighten their self-awareness through card interpretation.

The major arcana sequence tells not only the Fool's story but also ours, because the Fool is within us all. When we read tarot, we are the Fool finding our way. We meet the archetypes, or templates, of human character and experience, which help us explore the deepest desires and motivations of others and ourselves.

The shape of 0 in the Fool signifies the egg, for potential, and in the World, wholeness and cycles.

THE FOOL'S JOURNEY IN CARDS

At 0, the Fool begins their adventure with a step into thin air and a heart full of dreams. On meeting I The Magician, they discover the Pentacle, Cup, Wand, and Sword, the four elements of the universe. The Fool might have had these tools in their knapsack all along, but it takes meeting the sorcerer to know them.

Next, the Fool needs to understand why they must go on this adventure, and they encounter II The High Priestess, a wise woman who helps them connect with their intuition. Next, III The Empress shows the Fool how to nurture their idea, and IV The Emperor shows them how to bring order to their thoughts. Next, V The High Priest gives them counsel, and the Fool begins to sense the role they might play in wider society. They meet a partner in card VI The Lovers and must decide whether to leave or commit to them. At VII The Chariot, the Fool is ready to take to the road, driven by determination rather than understanding.

With VIII Strength, the Fool learns a lesson. Although they have become a warrior, or charioteer, the maiden demonstrates that gentleness is also power. Next, IX The Hermit teaches the Fool about nurturing their inner light and finding the path of spirituality alone. At X The Wheel of Fortune, the halfway point of the journey, the Fool realizes that not everything is within their power; the universe has its own agenda.

0
The Fool:
Risk, opportunity,
beginnings

I
The Magician:
Action, resourcefulness,
manifesting

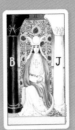

II
The High Priestess:
Learning, intuition,
discretion

III
The Empress:
Creativity, productivity,
abundance

IV
The Emperor:
Order, stability,
organization

V
The Hierophant:
Unity, religion, education

VI
The Lovers:
Love, decisions, maturity

VII
The Chariot:
Travel, determination,
energy

VIII
Strength:
Patience, resilience, strength

IX
The Hermit:
Contemplation, esoteric
learning, inner guidance

X
The Wheel of Fortune:
Fate, destiny, flow

At XI Justice, the Fool comes up against society's opinions of them. With XII The Hanged Man, the Fool undergoes a spiritual initiation—they sense they must sacrifice old ways of seeing, which culminates in XIII Death and the demise of the Fool's old self. They must leave behind their old values, seeking higher guidance in the form of the Temperance's angel at card XIV. With XV The Devil, the Fool's shadow emerges, and they must know their own darkness in order to be free. This process completes with XVI The Tower, when the Fool surrenders control to higher forces.

The Fool finds hope in card XVII The Star, which lights their way onward. With XVIII The Moon, the Fool learns discernment and, now aware of higher realities, must make wise choices. Entering the garden of XIX The Sun, symbol of full consciousness, success, and growth, the Fool rests and prepares for the final stages of their journey; here, they reclaim their joyful inner child. With XX Judgment, the Fool finally reviews their past, dealing with guilt and memories, forgiving themself and others so that they may progress to XXI The World, symbol of expansion and completion, at which point their soul ascends. They become one with the universe and are reborn at 0; and so the cycle begins again.

XI
Justice:
Fairness, balance, decisions

XII
The Hanged Man:
Waiting, perspective,
sacrifice

XIII
Death:
Endings, transformation,
truth

XIV
Temperance:
Balance, responsibility,
alchemy, guidance

XV
The Devil:
Entrapment, self-sabotage,
temptation

XVI
The Tower:
Disaster, surrender,
enlightenment

XVII
The Star:
Renewal, healing, hope

XVIII
The Moon:
The past, mysteries,
uncertainty

XIX
The Sun:
Joy, protection, growth,
children

XX
Judgment:
Awakening, reviewing,
second chances

XXI
The World:
Success, completion,
expansion, travel

THE THREE STAGES OF THE FOOL'S JOURNEY

The Fool's Journey can be understood to be in three stages, with seven cards in each.

1 — I The Magician to VII The Chariot: Formative Encounters

This first stage concerns the Fool in the material world. This familiar world is family, relationships, and society (some see the Empress and Emperor as the Fool's parents). The Fool has gathered information from each person they have encountered, and they have begun to make decisions about which direction to take. By the last card, VII The Chariot, the Fool is ready to leave the world they know.

2 — VIII Strength to XIV Temperance: Innocence to Experience

The second stage shows the Fool in the realm of the mind. The Fool must tested so they grow in experience. Each of the cards in this stage introduce the Fool to the questions of morality, rules, and responsibility, and they discover more about themself through each trial. By the last card, XIV Temperance, the Fool has released their old self and meets a higher form of consciousness in the form of Temperance's Archangel Michael.

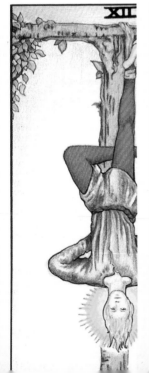

3 — XV The Devil to XXI The World: Evolution and Ascension

The final stage sees the Fool on the path toward spiritual ascension. The experiences represented by this sequence of seven, from the Devil's fear and entrapment to freedom in the Sun, bring the Fool to oneness with the universe, expressed by the final card, XXI The World. Their soul's journey is complete. The Fool now returns to the world, reincarnated as the beginner all over again.

READING THE MAJORS BY NUMBERS

The cards' numbers can reveal the position you're in and the likely outcome. For this spread, we use the cards' numbers to see how a situation might progress. The lower the major arcana card, the younger the situation. The higher the number, the more developed the situation and the closer to the end of a phase or cycle. You can apply this technique to any scenario, including relationships. The readings use six major arcana cards, so begin by separating the majors from the minors.

Career by Numbers

Working with only the major arcana cards, formulate your career question. You might ask, "What stage am I at in my career?" or "Am I coming to the end of this job and do I need to look for work?" or "Is this new role right for me?" Shuffle your question into your cards, choose three (see page 15), and place them in a row, facedown. Now turn all three over and see which majors you have.

Here's the reading Jed got. He loved his new job at a start-up, but he wondered whether the company—and his job—would last.

From the first three cards, we see that Jed has joined this start-up toward the end of a cycle. The Sun is card XIX, which is close to the last card, the World. Judgment suggests that the company will shortly be under financial review, and he has a feeling that more investment will be needed if he is to keep his job. He has joined the company just before some vital financial decisions, which will result in a new cycle of investment or, potentially, closure. VI The Lovers, with its lower number, advises that time is on his side. Jed could leave (and find it relatively easy to find a role in another company). To investigate, we laid a second row of three cards:

We began with XIX The Sun on the first row of cards, so the Devil as card XV is a backward step. It appears that there will be some new restrictions to deal with—perhaps budgets or staff will be reduced—but I The Magician takes us to a positive new beginning. The company will need to use the resources it does have more efficiently. At a personal level, the card advises Jed to focus on his skills and contribution rather than the future of the company. The Emperor as card IV predicts stability, which could suggest a better management and financial structure, so the outlook is optimistic.

Of course, there are many ways to interpret these cards, but this example shows how to use the card's number as an effective starting point for your reading.

Love by Numbers

You can use the same majors—only spread as above for love and relationships, again choosing two sets of three cards and interpreting them by their numbers.

Shuffle your love question into your cards and choose your first three (see page 15). Interpret those, then lay your next three, again focusing on the numbers on the cards and whether they are low, midrange, or high.

Celine wanted to look at the future of her relationship. These were her cards:

The Fool as 0 and VII The Chariot show a new relationship that developed quickly but burned out, indicated by XVI The Tower. Is it retrievable? The next three cards show a step backward, from XVI to XII The Hanged Man, and another retreat denoted by IX The Hermit. Celine needs time to reconsider the relationship. The Tower symbolizes drama and endings—their love connection may have felt powerful but could also be destructive. Judgment at card XX sees a move forward, as there's an upcoming opportunity to give the relationship a second chance. And it feels all or nothing; they either start again together or go their separate ways.

NUMBER REFLECTIONS

In this section, you'll see how to quickly unlock the secrets of the major arcana through their numerical connections. Major cards grouped under numbers 1 through 9 are referred to as reflections because their meanings are interrelated.

This might sound complex, but it's remarkably simple. Each pair or trio of cards in a group shares the same reduced number, which is always between 1 and 9. A reduced number is the single digit you get by adding together the numbers you see on your card.

For example, for XXI The World, we take XXI as 21, then add the 2 to the 1 to give 3 ($2 + 1 = 3$). So, the reduced number of the World is 3 (III). The Empress is also III, so the World and the Empress fall under the number 3. The Hanged Man, card XII, or 12, also reduces to 3. The energy of 3 is creative, so creativity and growth play a part in the interpretation of all three cards.

What About the Fool?

Note that the Fool isn't included in these groupings. The Fool's number is 0, which signifies the void from which life emerges. But we do see his 0 in 10 The Wheel of Fortune and in 20 Judgment. These two cards signify what is unseen: The Wheel symbolizes cosmic forces beyond our control, while Judgment evokes memories and the world of spirit. The Fool and their 0 represent what is in our awareness but not manifest in physical form.

At a Glance

REDUCED NUMBER   MAJOR ARCANA GROUP

1. . . . . Magician, Wheel of Fortune, Sun

2. . . . . High Priestess, Justice, Judgment

3. . . . . Empress, Hanged Man, World

4. . . . . Emperor, Death

5. . . . . Hierophant, Temperance

6. . . . . Lovers, Devil

7. . . . . Chariot, Tower

8. . . . . Strength, Star

9. . . . . Hermit, Moon

Number 1

One signifies beginnings, new cycles, energy, spiritual awareness, and divine intelligence. Its ruling planet is the Sun, and its element is Fire. Three major arcana cards come under number 1:

I • The Magician: 1

Key meanings: *Beginnings, action, creativity, success, resources, manifesting*

The Magician is about to manifest what they desire from thin air. Magic has begun. Also note the number 8 as the lemniscate, or infinity symbol, above the Magician's head.

X • The Wheel of Fortune: 1 (1 + 0 = 1)

Key meanings: *Fate, change, cycles, intuition*

The Wheel of Fortune heralds a new era of understanding. We begin to appreciate forces beyond our knowing or control and attune to the flow of life and luck.

XIX • The Sun: 1 (1 + 9 = 10; 1 + 0 = 1)

Key meanings: *Optimism, growth, happiness, health*

The Sun shows joy and spiritual growth after the darkness of the preceding card, the Moon. The child of the Sun begins their journey toward the World and spiritual ascension.

Number 2

Two represents duality and partnership. It's about the relationship between 1 and 1, which may be complementary or oppositional, creating harmony or tension. Two's ruling planet is the Moon, and its element is Water. Three major arcana cards come under number 2:

II · The High Priestess: 2

Key meanings: *Psychic work, intuition, spiritual knowledge, secrets, discernment*

The High Priestess lives in two worlds, the earthly and the celestial. She navigates both with wisdom and discretion.

XI · Justice: 2 (1 + 1 = 2)

Key meanings: *Justice, fairness, retribution, balance*

Justice, as the judge, must use discernment to mete out retribution or show mercy. Justice says that, on balance, we will be treated fairly by others.

XX · Judgment: 2 (2 + 0 = 2)

Key meanings: *Review, memories, spiritual awakening*

Judgment also relies on discernment, as it invites us to assess our past actions. We may need to appreciate our work or forgive ourselves or others to move on.

Number 3

Three is the number of creation. It represents outcomes, energy, creative power, and fulfillment. Its ruling planet is Jupiter, and its element is Fire. Three major arcana cards come under number 3:

III · The Empress: 3

Key meanings: *Creativity, abundance, growth*

The Empress is the earth mother who gives life; 3 represents the child (the outcome of the relationship of 2). The Empress symbolizes creativity, fertility, and abundance.

XII · The Hanged Man: 3 (1 + 2 = 3)

Key meanings: *Spiritual initiation, new perspectives, sacrifice, compromise*

The Hanged Man stands for spiritual incubation, just as the pregnant Empress incubates a child. His reward, or outcome, is perspective and vision.

XXI · The World: 3 (2 + 1 = 3)

Key meanings: *Success, completion, expansion, travel, celebration*

The World, card of completion and expansion, integrates three aspects of the self—the mind, body, and spirit—to bring wholeness.

Number 4

Four is the number of stability. It's associated with support, order, and balance. In Pythagorean numerology (see page 10), 4 denoted truth and justice. Four's ruling planet is Uranus, and its element is Air. Two major arcana cards come under number 4:

IV • The Emperor: 4

Key meanings: *Order, stability, leadership*

The Emperor is the ruler, symbol of authority and order. He creates stability—the meaning of number 4—and establishes rules. The card also stands for protection and firm boundaries.

XIII • Death: 4 (1 + 3 = 4)

Key meanings: *Change, release, truth, transformation, beginnings*

Death is change that we must accept; it is the outcome of truth. Things may be taken from us so that new opportunities can arise. The Emperor rebuilds after Death's work is done, bringing peace and order after disruption.

Number 5

Five is the number of human experience, tests, spiritual growth, and togetherness. As the sum of 3, a male number, and 2, a female number, 5 was once thought of as the number of marriage. Five's ruling planet is Mercury, and its element is Air. Two major arcana cards come under number 5:

V · The Hierophant: 5

Key meanings: *Unity, togetherness, education, learning, marriage*

The Hierophant communicates the word of God as teaching. A conduit between heaven and earth, they stand for unity and learning. Historically, the card meant marriage.

XIV · Temperance: 5 (1 + 4 = 5)

Key meanings: *Balance, alchemy, higher guidance, flow*

Temperance also reveals higher guidance in the form of Archangel Michael. Both the Hierophant and Archangel Michael mediate between spirit/ God and humankind.

Number 6

Six is the number of love, harmony, and peace. As the sum of 1, 2, and 3, it signifies outcomes. Comprising three 2s, 6 also symbolizes partnerships and people close to us. Six's ruling planet is Venus, and its element is Earth. Two major arcana cards come under number 6:

VI · The Lovers: 6

Key meanings: *Love, a mature decision*

The Lovers reveal love and partnership in paradise—the perfection of number 6—but also the need for a mature decision.

XV · The Devil: 6 (1 + 5 = 6)

Key meanings: *Temptation, lust, entrapment, affairs, addiction, self-conflict*

The Devil is the Lovers' shadow. Archangel Raphael becomes the devil, and the two lovers have grown demon horns. If they break free, they can return to paradise to make their own choices.

Number 7

Seven, the highest single-digit prime number, stands for mysteries, potential, and intuition. Comprising stable 3 and creative 4, the number 7 can also symbolize wisdom. Seven's ruling planet is Neptune, and its element is Water. Two major arcana cards come under number 7:

VII · The Chariot: 7

Key meanings: *Travel, progress, determination, moving*

The Chariot forges ahead, full of determination. Because 7 is a number of potential, the card says we are driven toward our goal. To travel safely, we must temper our ego with practicality.

XVI · The Tower: 7 (1 + 6 = 7)

Key meanings: *Natural forces, disaster, surrender, enlightenment*

The Tower symbolizes collapse. This may be a collapse of the ego, a way of living, or even a physical structure. Destruction clears the way for the new and offers unforeseen opportunities for renewal and positive change. The twenty-two gold droplets are formed in the shape of the Hebrew letter Yod, which signifies the divine hand of God.

Number 8

Eight symbolizes transformation and regeneration. Additional meanings include manifesting and dedication; two stable 4s in combination suggest a determination to create change. Eight's ruling planet is Saturn, and its element is Earth. Two major arcana cards come under number 8:

VIII · Strength: 8

Key meanings: *Strength, wellness, patience, values, standing your ground*

Strength offers hope and inner strength. The number 8 appears as the lemniscate, or infinity symbol, above the maiden's head.

XVII · The Star: 8 (1 + 7 = 8)

Key meanings: *Hope, inspiration, healing, renewal, guidance*

The Star has eight stars in the sky above the star maiden, and each star has eight points. The meaning of the symbolism of 8 in both cards is the renewal of energy.

Number 9

Nine stands for pressure before release. Comprising three 3s, 9 has an intensity that often brings an alternative reality. This tension is resolved when we reach number 10, which stands for completion. Nine's ruling planet is Mars, and its element is Fire. Two major arcana cards come under number 9:

IX • The Hermit: 9

Key meanings: *Contemplation, meditation, time alone, esoteric learning, self-healing*

The Hermit depicts the number 9 as culmination; the Hermit has shed their worldly possessions in order to find their purpose.

XVIII • The Moon: 9 (1 + 8 = 9)

Key meanings: *Mysteries, dreams, illusion, past issues, intuition, soul work*

The Moon may illuminate or deceive. The intensity of the number 9 is depicted in the vulnerability of the crayfish, unsure whether it can trust its instincts to leave the safety of the pool. The fifteen gold droplets represent thought, and they are formed in the shape of the Hebrew letter Yod, which signifies the divine hand of God. Both cards suggest a solitary path—the Hermit on the snowy mountaintop and the lost soul, as the crayfish, trying to find its way through an unknown, half-lit terrain.

2

THE MINOR ARCANA CARDS BY NUMBERS

In this chapter, we look at suit elements and numbers, see how numbers Ace through Ten symbolize a journey, and explore the meanings of the sixteen Court cards. You'll find a spread to try for each number, too.

MINOR ARCANA NUMBERS

Minor arcana means "small secrets." The fifty-six minor cards show us the details of our lives and are arranged into four suits: Cups, Pentacles, Swords, and Wands. In each fourteen-card suit, four cards are known as Court cards—Page, Knight, Queen, and King (in some decks, the Page is titled Knave or Princess). The remaining cards, Ace through Ten, are referred to as number cards or pip cards. The word *pip* comes from the motifs on playing cards—the hearts, spades, diamonds, and clubs, which relate to Cups, Swords, Pentacles, and Wands, respectively.

Minor Arcana Number Meanings at a Glance

Ones (Aces):
Beginnings, energy

Twos:
*Partnership, attraction,
balance, tension*

Threes:
*Creativity, expression,
acknowledgment*

Fours:
*Stability, protection,
boundaries*

Fives:
*Instability, changes,
experience*

Sixes:
*Harmony, improvement,
stage of completion or
realization*

Sevens:
*Potential, ambitions,
the unknown*

Eights:
Change, rewards, progress

Nines:
Intensity, accumulation

Tens:
*Completion, endings,
beginnings*

Looking at the numbers from Ace through Ten, we can understand the number sequence as a journey. Ace is the beginning and Ten is the completion; the intervening numbers denote the stages of the journey, which becomes expansive (Two and Three), then stable and reflective (Four). There are tests at Five, stages of success or resolution at Six, and new potential and challenges with Seven. Eight brings change and reward, Nine brings an accumulation of experience, and the final Ten reveals the journey's outcome.

For example, with Cups, suit of the heart, we can see the card sequence as a relationship journey (see opposite).

In this way, the card numbers represent stages of experience in the form of a story. As the numbers go higher, life unfolds further.

A Relationship Journey

Ace of Cups:
The beginning. A new love.

Two of Cups:
Two people. Partnership and commitment.

Three of Cups:
Expression of love. Joy.

Four of Cups:
Stability that may turn to boredom. Doubt.

Five of Cups:
Change and challenges to the relationship.

Six of Cups:
Harmony restored.

Seven of Cups:
Unknown factors. Is the relationship sustainable or based on fantasy?

Eight of Cups:
The point of further commitment or departure.

Nine of Cups:
Happiness shared. Wishes fulfilled.

Ten of Cups:
Love and expansion. A dream home.

THE FOUR SUITS AND THEIR ELEMENTS

Each minor arcana suit has an associated element—Earth, Air, Fire, or Water. The element of a suit tells us about a suit's nature, or essential characteristics.

Cups:
Element of Water.
Emotions, relationships.
The realm of the heart.

Pentacles:
Element of Earth.
Property, money, work, achievement.
The material realm, including
the body.

Swords:
Element of Air.
The intellect, decisions, conflicts.
The realm of the mind.

Wands:
Element of Fire.
Instinct, passion,
communication, travel.
The realm of the soul.

PUTTING IT TOGETHER: FINDING MEANING

To divine the meaning of a minor arcana card, consider the card's symbols, suit and element, and number. These aspects of a card work together like magic to create meaning. The key issue is that the meaning of a number changes according to the suit, so we must combine what we know about a suit's element with the meaning of the number. This may sound complex, but once you're familiar with the suits and their elements and what the numbers mean, you'll soon begin to glean meaning for your cards during a reading. Rather than stop and refer to a book, you'll develop the confidence to interpret your cards in the moment.

Here's an example.

Four of Wands:
In the suit of Wands with its element of Fire, the Four is positive because it stabilizes fire and creates boundaries. So, the Four of Wands shows freedom and protection; two figures celebrate in a sunny garden.

Four of Pentacles:
In the suit of Pentacles, we have the ultra-stable Four with the element of Earth, which is equally grounded. But the two together suggest that we may be too comfortable in materialism, shown by the male figure grasping his coin.

Four of Swords:
In the suit of Swords with its element of Air, stable Four brings respite from conflict. The knight in the chapel has laid down his arms.

Four of Cups:
In the emotional suit of Cups with its Water element, the stable Four brings feelings to a halt. Water needs to flow, and still water can become stagnant—hence the listless figure under the tree, bored and withdrawn.

NUMBER AS PATTERN: READING MOTIF MINORS

Early tarot decks such as the Visconti Sforza and Marseilles tarots have motif minor cards; Ace through Ten were illustrated with Coins, Wands, Cups, and Swords motifs rather than pictures depicting a scene. From this, we know that many tarot readers (and indeed readers of playing cards) before us knew how to interpret numbers without elaborate visual cues. Their knowledge to some degree would have been based on seeing number as pattern, and the leap between these patterns, from one number to the next, as a story.

Here's an example.

When we look at four, the number alone suggests stability. The four motifs are even and balanced, like the four corners of a house or a chair. It's a neat group. But when we get to five, there's suddenly an extra element to contend with. There are now two groups of two, with a lone coin in the center creating this separation. Will one group dominate the other? In this way, we can see the Five of Coins, or Pentacles, as imbalance and potential isolation. In the Five of Cups we find sadness, or imbalance of emotion. The Five of Wands reveals a test of stability, and the Five of Swords indicates loss and humiliation.

The pattern of five suit motifs on a card, therefore, suggests transition, a necessary rite of passage before we can arrive at the even, harmonious six. The kind of transition we can expect is revealed by the card's suit.

THE ACES

The Ace in the minor arcana signifies beginnings and energy. Ace as number one has the shape of a rod or wand, which tells us that the minor arcana Aces deal with manifesting: An idea or ideal is born. On the Rider Waite Smith cards, the suit symbol appears in a hand from a cloud as if gifting us with the highest potential of its element.

Ace of Cups:
A new relationship or other passion; falling in love and overflowing emotion. The card may also mean pregnancy. The twenty-six droplets are formed in the shape of the Hebrew letter Yod, which signifies the divine hand of God.

Ace of Pentacles:
Money comes with success: a new home or job, business project, or creative venture.

Ace of Swords:
A strong decision brings victory and a new start. A breakthrough in thinking. The six droplets symbolize divine grace, as for the Ace of Cups.

Ace of Wands:
Motivation and drive. Adventures, travel, communication, and ideas gather pace. The card is also a symbol of male fertility.

What's Beginning?

In this spread, we draw together the powerful energy of the four Aces and their associated directions to assist the reading:

North: Earth, suit of Pentacles

South: Fire, suit of Wands

East: Air, suit of Swords

West: Water, suit of Cups

The fifth element of Spirit is represented in the center of the four Aces, which is where you will place one card.

First, place the four Aces faceup. Next, put the remaining minor arcana cards to one side, leaving only the majors. Shuffle the majors as you ask, "What's beginning?" or "What new influences are coming?" Choose one card and place it facedown in the center. Take a breath, then turn the card faceup.

To interpret your card, say the answer to your question out loud, beginning with "A time for . . ." For example, if you got the Hermit as your center card, this would be "A time for contemplation." For III The Empress, you might say, "Time to be productive" (or for some, "Time to get pregnant"). XV The Devil suggests that a time of restriction is coming, so there may be something you can do now to avoid that—changing your mind about a commitment, for example. (See also the directory of card meanings on pages 162 to 171.)

Ace of Pentacles

Ace of Cups

Ace of Swords

Ace of Wands

THE TWOS

The Twos in the minor arcana signify partnership, attraction, balance, and tension. The Twos also stand for duality, in which two contrasting states—such as light and shade—coexist. This duality may be harmonious or may create tension and conflict. Therefore, these cards deal with partnership and decision-making. As it takes two to have a conversation, the Twos also represent the importance of communication.

Two of Cups: A love commitment; recognizing a soul mate and nurturing that relationship. A card of love and peace.

Two of Pentacles: Decisions concerning money and cash flow. More broadly, choosing between two viable options.

Two of Swords: An unresolved situation; time out or a truce. The card can also show procrastination and the need for a clear decision.

Two of Wands: All types of partnerships flourish. Time to make plans, particularly around travel and creative projects.

The Decision

In this spread, we work with the Two of Pentacles as a symbol of decision-making. The Rider Waite Smith card shows a man juggling two coins, which form the shape of a figure eight or lemniscate (as shown on the opposite page and below). This signifies going backward and forward trying to make up your mind.

Place the Two of Coins faceup in the center. Now shuffle all the remaining cards, both minors and majors, as you allow your question to flow through your hands and into the cards. Visualize option 1, then option 2, and slow your breathing as you do, so you begin to feel more open and relaxed. Try not to invest any emotion in the outcome of the reading; be willing to see what the cards show.

When you are ready, take two cards from the top of the deck and place them as shown, facedown. Then turn over your cards and interpret them in turn.

Option 1   Option 2

Example: Your cards offer insight into the nature of each choice. Option 1, the Six of Swords, shows this choice is an escape route. Option 2 is the Four of Wands, which shows freedom and celebration. The message is not to jump on the first or easiest path (option 1). It offers short-term relief after a time of struggle, but option 2 appears to offer more in terms of personal reward.

THE THREES

The Threes in the minor arcana embrace creativity, expression, truth, and acknowledgment. Three means an outcome (the synergy of Two), so we now have a tangible result—from the togetherness of the Three of Cups to the sorrow of the Three of Swords.

Three of Cups:
Joy and celebration.

Three of Pentacles:
Early success.

Three of Swords:
Sorrow and heartbreak. The truth surfaces. Betrayal.

Three of Wands:
Plans in action. Travel, communication, good relationships with others.

What's My Future at Work?

Take out the Three of Pentacles to represent work and productivity, placing it faceup in the center. Next, shuffle the whole deck and consider the work you do and where it may lead you. You can work with this spread to look at creative projects, too. When you are ready, choose three cards (see page 15) and lay them facedown in the positions shown. Give yourself a moment to feel centered and open to what the cards may show you before turning them faceup.

3
The next step

1
My work situation now

2
How others see my work

When you interpret your cards, pay particular attention to card 1, your work situation. This card can reveal how you feel about your work or even your occupation. For example, the Ace of Cups in this position is saying you love your work—although you may get over-involved, as it's a card of the heart. Alternatively, you may get a card that is literal, such as Justice for work in the legal profession. Card 2 gives you the view of others (which may or may not influence how you see your work situation), and card 3 is an advice card, offering a potential way to develop your current career or even begin a new career path. You can pull more cards around card 3 for more information, too.

THE FOURS

Fours in the minor arcana mean stability. Depending on the suit, this stability comes in the form of retreat, joy, or boredom. While it represents a welcome or necessary pause for some, it can suggest underlying restlessness, which becomes evident in the unbalanced Five. Stability gives us comfort, but it may not meet all our needs for fulfillment.

Four of Cups: Boredom. A feeling of dissatisfaction. Not knowing which direction to take.

Four of Pentacles: Financial stability, but a tendency toward materialism. Self-reliance.

Four of Swords: Necessary time out from work; a relationship or decision on hold.

Four of Wands: Joy and celebration. A sense of freedom and love.

What Can I Do to Get This Situation Moving?

Remove all the major arcana cards from the deck, leaving just the minors.
Take out the Four of Swords, which represents the situation that is on hold,
and place it faceup in the center. Then shuffle the remaining minors and
lay four cards facedown.

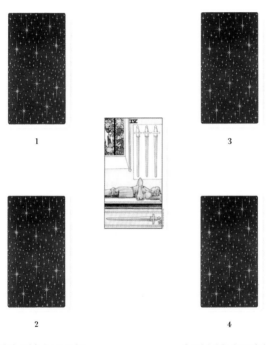

| Cards 1 and 2: Reasons for | 3 and 4: What's needed to |
| this situation | move on |

To interpret your cards, first look at the balance of suits (see page 50):
Do you have lots of Swords cards with no Cups, or a split of Pentacles and
Wands? For example, more Swords cards would say that the reason for the
situation could be in the mind—perhaps feeling overloaded with problems—
but that equally, what's needed is to think differently. A quick survey of suits
acts as your starting point for your reading, after which you can interpret the
cards individually.

THE FIVES

Five in the minor arcana is the number of human experience. From a place of stability, the Four, we encounter uneven Five. The number Five upsets the balance, bringing personal challenges to our sense of security. These come as potential trials, battles, loss, and isolation. However, the message is that it's not what happens but how you manage it. There is hope.

Five of Cups:
Sadness and a
sense of loss.
Self-protection.

Five of Pentacles:
Financial stress
and fear of lack.
Fear of isolation.

Five of Swords:
Defeat and
potential
humiliation in
an unwinnable
battle. Bullying.

Five of Wands:
Tests and trials.
A battle of egos;
the need for others
to listen.

Why Am I Being Tested?

Place the Five of Wands, which symbolizes present struggles and tests, faceup in the center. Then shuffle the remainder of the deck (see page 13), letting your situation arise in your mind, and lay five cards facedown. The cards make the shape of V, the Roman numeral for Five. Take a moment to settle, then turn the cards faceup and begin your interpretation.

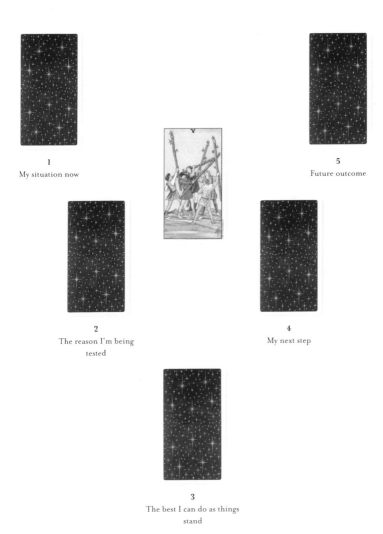

1
My situation now

5
Future outcome

2
The reason I'm being
tested

4
My next step

3
The best I can do as things
stand

When you look at all your cards together, you begin to see beyond your situation and, for a time, step back from any sense of unrest. Pay particular attention to card 3, which reveals what action or approach brings clarity.

THE SIXES

The Sixes in the minor arcana represent harmony and expansion. This sense of serenity derives from stable Four, coupled with balanced Two; equally, it's the sum of two Threes, or two cycles of creativity. Six also signifies a stage of completion on the minor arcana journey—there is now time to appreciate success or simply find peace after stress. In this way, all the Sixes are positive.

Six of Cups:
Happy memories.
A visitor arrives
bringing
friendship and
affection. A gift.

Six of Pentacles:
Generosity. Money
coming to you
or that you give
to others.

Six of Swords:
Moving on from
conflict to a place
of peace within,
or to a physical
location away
from strife.

Six of Wands:
Success and
acknowledgment,
particularly in
examinations
and tests.

Gratitude

This layout is based around the Six of Cups, card of memory and harmony. This is a helpful spread when you need an uplift, and it may also help you work toward forgiveness by appreciating the positives in a person or a past situation that may not have worked out as you had hoped.

Place the Six of Cups in the center faceup, then shuffle the remaining deck as you open your mind. You don't need to consciously generate a feeling of gratitude; the cards will help you do this. Just allow a feeling of trust and calmness to flow. Then, when you are ready, choose three cards (see page 15) and place them facedown.

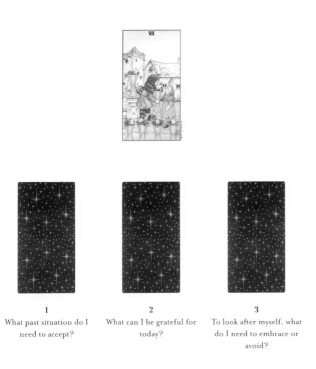

1	2	3
What past situation do I need to accept?	What can I be grateful for today?	To look after myself, what do I need to embrace or avoid?

This is a great spread to do with a friend—you can read for yourself as your companion listens, then adds their interpretation of your cards. This process often helps you remember positives in your life that may not be apparent to you just now.

THE SEVENS

The number Seven in the minor arcana represents potential. A surfeit of possibilities, however, can be destabilizing. We can overthink or lose focus, so Seven asks us to consider our next steps and direct our energy carefully. The message of Seven across the suits is to choose wisely, avoiding distraction.

Seven of Cups:
Choices; needing more information as there are many possibilities. Living in a fantasy world.

Seven of Pentacles:
Great potential, but work needs to continue to secure future success.

Seven of Swords:
Displacement. Missing items or ideas or opportunities being stolen. Underhanded behavior.

Seven of Wands:
Standing up for your beliefs and/ or those of others. Anticipating problems and challenges; defending your ground.

How Do I Stay Focused?

The Seven of Pentacles represents the need to stay focused on a goal. The shape of number 7 resembles a rake or garden hoe, a symbol of the need to keep tending your projects so they grow to their fullest potential.

Take out the Seven of Pentacles and place it faceup. Now visualize your project as you shuffle the remainder of the deck. Does the path ahead feel smooth, or do you sense a block? Your cards will show you how you might proceed. Now lay three cards facedown as shown.

| 1 | 2 | 3 |
| How you're dealing with this situation now | What needs to happen next | The likely outcome |

When interpreting your cards, you may find that your card 2 does not suggest any action—for example, if you got the Two or Four of Swords or the Four of Cups. This may mean you need to rest and step back before you make a decision. In one reading of the spread, I saw the Four of Swords as card 2 followed by the Ace of Swords as card 3; time out to rest (Four of Swords) leads to a breakthrough (Ace of Swords) and a decisive way forward.

THE EIGHTS

The number Eight in the minor arcana symbolizes change, cycles, and movement. The sideways 8 as the infinity symbol or lemniscate stands for life as a continual cycle (see this symbol on I The Magician and VIII Strength, pages 35 and 42). The minor arcana Eights, therefore, deal with change, cycles, and adjustment.

Eight of Cups: A change of heart. The emotional work is done; a quiet departure, a moving on.

Eight of Pentacles: Success and self-appreciation. The end of a cycle of learning; new opportunities begin to unfold.

Eight of Swords: Restriction and circular thinking. A change in attitude brings freedom.

Eight of Wands: Speed, communication, and transition. Adjusting to a faster pace until the situation stabilizes.

How Do I Make a Change?

In this spread, we work with the Eight of Cups as a symbol of change. This card denotes change in the emotions. However, if you prefer, you can choose another Eight to align with the change you'd like to see: Take out the Eight of Pentacles for work or education, the Eight of Swords for conflict and decisions, or the Eight of Wands if you'd like more—or less!—fire energy in your life.

Place your chosen Eight faceup in the center. Take a moment to contemplate the card's image: How does it make you feel? You may find that the card brings to mind your personal challenge. Ask your cards for guidance as you shuffle all of them (both major and minor arcana). Take three cards from the top of the deck and place them facedown. When you are ready, turn over your cards and interpret them in turn.

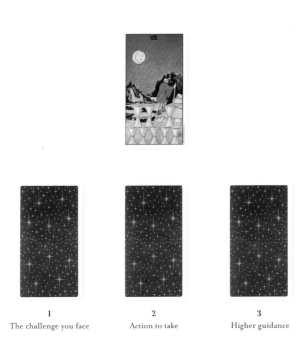

1	2	3
The challenge you face	Action to take	Higher guidance

In one reading, card 1 was the Six of Swords and card 2 the Nine of Swords. How could the anxious Nine be interpreted as "action to take"? It felt as if card 2, here, explained card 1: Moving away from a situation (the Six) because of the stress it caused (the Nine). If you have a similar experience in your reading, follow your intuition: Group cards 1 and 2 together, move card 3 into the card 2 position, and take another card from the deck as your new card 3. Of course, you can stick with the original card—but in this instance, moving the cards along opened up new possibilities for the reading.

THE NINES

Comprising three sets of dynamic Three, Nine is the number of intensity. All the minor arcana Nines show figures in enclosed areas, which conveys a sense of containment. The Nines must contain the power of their element—all the burdens and joys of the journey that began with the Ace—until the release of the Ten.

Nine of Cups:
The tarot "wish" card. Luck and manifesting; what you wish for becomes possible. Generosity and sharing.

Nine of Pentacles:
Contentment and security. A nurturing environment; time for you.

Nine of Swords:
Anxiety and stress. Disturbance, nightmares; overthinking.

Nine of Wands:
A strong position. Self-protection due to past challenges. A need to heal from an old wound.

What Can I Manifest?

In this spread, we take the Nine of Cups as our focus: This is the "wish" card of the tarot, for manifestation. Take the Nine from the deck and place it faceup in the center, as shown. Take a moment to reflect on the card and ask: What am I manifesting? What can I manifest now?

When you are ready, shuffle the whole deck, holding these questions in mind. Lay four cards from the top of the pile facedown, as shown, then turn them faceup.

1
Past experience

3
Next wish

2
What I'm manifesting now

4
Potential outcome

To interpret your cards, see them in two groups: cards 1 and 2 for the past and present and cards 3 and 4 for the present and future. If cards 3 and 4 are not what you hope—for example, they may reveal stress (Nine of Swords) or tests (Five of Wands)—you can do a little tarot magic by changing your cards. Remove cards 3 and 4 from the spread, and look through the remaining deck of cards faceup. Consider what you truly want and what will bring you happiness. Then choose new cards 3 and 4 and place them back in the spread. This action signals that you are ready to manifest what you want and that you trust yourself and the universe to make that wish come true.

THE TENS

Ten is the number of resolution, wholeness, and completion. Within number 10 is the 1, for initiation, and 0, for wholeness and rebirth. Zero, number of the Fool (see page 34), takes the form of an egg, symbol of new life.

Ten of Cups:
Happiness, love, and stability. A new home. Sharing love.

Ten of Pentacles:
Wealth and security. A wedding. Support from others within a biological or chosen family.

Ten of Swords:
A swift ending; the end of a particular phase, or a job or relationship. Can also refer to the death of the old self so the new you can flourish.

Ten of Wands:
A burden; losing perspective due to overwork. Too many issues to contend with alone.

How Do I Move On?

We work with the Ten of Swords and the numbers 1 and 10. First, take out the Ten of Swords and place the card faceup. Then shuffle the remaining cards (see page 13) as you reflect on the situation you would like to move on from. When you are ready, take the first and tenth cards from the top of the deck.

10th Card:
What needs to be resolved
first

1st Card:
What outcome or
opportunity to expect

When interpreting the cards in this spread, try saying, "If I deal with [tenth card], then [first card] is the likely outcome." If you get cards that suggest stuckness or conflict as your outcome card, look again at your tenth card and consider its message in light of your situation. There may be an alternative approach you can take, or the card may suggest that this situation is better left alone; it may not be for you to resolve.

RECURRING NUMBERS

The following meanings for recurring number cards in a reading derive from Israel Regardie's *The Golden Dawn* (1940), a compendium of the philosophy and magical rites of the Hermetic Order of the Golden Dawn (see pages 81 and 83).

	FOUR	THREE
Aces	Great power and force	Riches and success
Twos	Conference and conversations	Reorganization
Threes	Resolution and determination	Deceit
Fours	Rest and peace	Industry
Fives	Order and regularity	Quarrels and fights
Sixes	Pleasure	Gain and success
Sevens	Disappointments	Treaties and compacts
Eights	Much news	Many journeys
Nines	Added responsibility	Much correspondence
Tens	Anxiety and responsibility	Buying, selling, and commercial transactions

COURT CARDS:
PEOPLE AND INFLUENCES

There are sixteen Court cards in a tarot deck—a Page, Knight, Queen, and King for each suit. Court cards can be people you know or people who are about to come into your life. To identify them, you might go by their appearance and likely occupation. The issue with this approach is that the traditional descriptions applied to Courts cannot be inclusive; Cups Courts, for example, were formerly described as "fair" and Pentacles as "dark." And the King of Pentacles, we're told, might work in agriculture or finance—so the profile we have is a dark, mature man who might be a farmer or banker.

In contemporary tarot readings, the Courts are not restricted to physical description or gender, and you may interpret them in whatever way feels right, including understanding Courts purely as influences. For example, let's say your querent (the person you are reading for), who identifies as female, has the King of Pentacles in her reading. The reading is focused on career. As an influence, this card represents financial authority and growth, so the querent is evolving into a King of Pentacles in her career. Equally, she may have a role model—a King of Pentacles who happens to be her (female) manager. So in this instance, the King of Pentacles operates on two levels, as an influence *and* a person. The card represents or literally embodies the querent's aspirations. This approach is important in tarot work; if you read every Court as a person and the querent can't relate to the people you describe, the reading comes to a standstill. Broaden your understanding of the Courts as influences, and you will find a new way into the energy of the reading.

For this reason, each Court card has two interpretations. The first is an influence in your life, and the second interpretation is how this influence may be expressed through the personality of someone you already know or may meet in the future.

For the reversed meanings of these cards, see page 166.

ETTEILLA'S HIERARCHY
OF COURTS

The famous French cartomancer Etteilla
(Jean-Baptiste Alliette, 1738–1791) gave these
broad meanings for the Court cards:

King:
Divine world (spirituality)

Queen:
Human world (vitality)

Knight:
Material world (materiality)

Knave (Page):
Transition stage; life passed on
The meaning for the Knave or Page as "transition stage"
can be interpreted as a fleeting influence, and "life passed on"
as a young person naturally benefiting from the wisdom passed
down to them.

PAGES

Pages are aligned with the element of Earth (see page 50). They represent young people or young situations across the four suits. For this reason, meanings of the Page include learning and transition, as a child or young person is in the process of growth toward adulthood (see box below). Pages can also mean news, bringing a new train of events.

	AS AN INFLUENCE:	AS A PERSON:
Page of Cups	*Fun, love, new friendship; developing sensitivity.*	*A young person who is perceptive and/or artistic.*
Page of Swords	*Taking care of the small details; new information.*	*A lively young person who is ambitious and conscientious.*
Page of Wands	*Good news about work, projects, and social activities.*	*A young person who is creative and talkative.*
Page of Pentacles	*New work, money, and educational opportunities.*	*A diligent young person who works hard for success.*

KNIGHTS

Knights are traditionally aligned with the element of Air; their alternative element is Fire (see page 50). Knights represent people, action, and situations in progress. An additional meaning of all the Knights is the material world (see Etteilla's Hierarchy of Courts, page 76); the Knights' actions have tangible outcomes.

	AS AN INFLUENCE:	AS A PERSON:
Knight of Cups	*An invitation or promise. Love on the horizon.*	*A dreamer; a romantic who represents an ideal.*
Knight of Swords	*Drama and discord. A stressful confrontation.*	*A fast-moving, ambitious individual who thrives on disruption.*
Knight of Wands	*Travel, culture, romance, moving home.*	*A charismatic networker.*
Knight of Pentacles	*Security and commitment. Financial planning.*	*A methodical, loyal individual who takes their time.*

QUEENS

Queens are aligned with the element of Water (see page 50). Queens represent mature people or mature situations. An additional association for the Queen is the human world (see box below). We can interpret this in terms of relationships, expression, and personal development.

	AS AN INFLUENCE:	AS A PERSON:
Queen of Cups	*Love, nurturing, and sensitivity.*	*A partner or potential partner. An intuitive, heart-centered individual.*
Queen of Swords	*Strength and insight. Discernment.*	*An astute and incisive thinker. A highly independent individual.*
Queen of Wands	*Growing self-worth. Self-expression, creativity, and energy*	*A communicative, inspirational individual.*
Queen of Pentacles	*Money and support. Love for the natural world.*	*A helper. An individual who is grounded and giving.*

KINGS

Kings are traditionally aligned with the element of Fire; their alternative element is Air (see page 50). As with the Queens, the Kings represent mature people or mature situations across the four suits. All four Kings may also be associated with the divine world or spirituality (see box below).

	AS AN INFLUENCE:	AS A PERSON:
King of Cups	*Love and support. Managing emotions.*	*A partner or potential partner who is wise and sensitive to others.*
King of Swords	*A clear decision. The need for strategic thinking.*	*A determined, ambitious character who may be ruthless.*
King of Wands	*Motivation and leadership. A time to show confidence.*	*A free spirit with charisma and vision.*
King of Pentacles	*Wealth and protection; money issues are resolved.*	*A generous and loyal individual.*

COURT CARDS AND ELEMENTS

As with cards Ace through Ten, the suit element of a Court card assists your interpretation. Yet Courts have a further element related to their status, or class, as Page, Knight, Queen, or King. Therefore, every Court card has two associated elements—one for their suit, and one for their class.

When you know a card's two elements, you'll find you begin to divine meanings during a reading. The Page of Pentacles, for example, is "Earth of Earth" because all Pages are Earth, and the suit of Pentacles is also Earth. The combination of two Earths as a character trait would indicate someone with strong practical and/or physical abilities, as Earth represents the body and the material world; this reflects the card's traditional meaning of a young person who works hard for success.

Golden Dawn Court Card Elements

	CUPS	PENTACLES	SWORDS	WANDS
Page	Earth of Water	Earth of Earth	Earth of Air	Earth of Fire
Knight	*Air of Water	Air of Earth	Air of Air	Air of Fire
Queen	Water of Water	Water of Earth	Water of Air	Water of Fire
King	*Fire of Water	Fire of Earth	Fire of Air	Fire of Fire

*Note that some contemporary tarotists prefer an alternative alignment of Knights as Fire and Kings as Air, given the action-driven Knights (Fire) and the strategic thinking required of the position of King.

COURT CARDS AND NUMBERS

In chapter 4, we will look at the quintessence card in a tarot spread; this is an additional card of advice that's calculated at the end of a reading by adding the numbers of all the cards in a spread and reducing to the number of a major arcana card (see page 130).

When divining the quintessence, some readers assign numbers to the Court cards—11 for Pages, 12 for Knights, 13 for Queens, and 14 for Kings—and add it to the other cards in the spread. So, if you had VI The Lovers, the Four of Pentacles, and the Queen of Cups, you would add 6 (Lovers) to 4 (Pentacles) to 13 (Queen of Cups): $6 + 4 + 13 = 23$. Then, $2 + 3 = 5$, for the Hierophant. Without including numbers for the Court cards, the calculation would be $6 + 4 = 10$ for the Wheel of Fortune. So, the quintessence card offers quite different guidance depending on the method used to determine it: The Wheel of Fortune invites us to go with the flow as luck will improve, while The Hierophant invites us to embrace our spiritual path through education and wise guidance. I generally omit numbers for Courts unless my small spread reveals only Court cards.

RECURRING COURT CARDS

The following meanings for recurring Court cards come from Israel Regardie's *The Golden Dawn*, see page 74.

	FOUR	THREE
Kings	Great swiftness	Unexpected meetings
Queens	Authority and influence	Powerful and influential friends
Knights	Meetings with important people	Rank and honor
Pages	New ideas and plans	The company of young people

3

TIMING
TECHNIQUES
AND INTUITION

In this chapter, you'll discover the timing
spreads for seeing ahead, timing techniques
that use the cards in your readings, and how to
work with a number as a symbol, which unlocks
even more messages in your cards.

TIMING AND ETHICS

The average timescale of a tarot reading is said to be between six and eighteen months. Yet the one question that arises over and again in readings is, "Yes, but *when* will this happen?" There are several techniques you can call upon to give likely timings for events, using spreads and your intuitive connection with a number; however, before you get started, there's a moral dimension to consider, too. One issue is that timings can become self-fulfilling for the recipient of the reading. If you suggest that romance will happen in three months' time, then this becomes absolute in that person's mind. They may not look for a partner until that time, or they might not recognize a soul mate who appears before that date. We have free will and are responsible for our lives and choices. You, as the tarot reader, do not become responsible for others' decisions, or for likely future events. What you can do is reveal the likely timing as you see it, with the caveat that timing is always fluid. You give the timings you have at the point of the reading, and many changes may occur after that time. A prediction, therefore, is the most likely occurrence of a future event as you sense it now; always explain this to whomever you are reading for.

For this or other reasons, you may not wish to give timings at all. But don't turn away from this chapter just yet: On pages 100 to 105, you will discover how to work with numbers not purely as a predictive tool but as symbols that enhance your intuition and open portals of wisdom in all your readings.

DAY AHEAD

This easy technique gives you a major arcana for the day ahead, plus an advice card. Add up today's date: day, month, and year. For example, for May 7, 2021, you would write the date as: 5 (May), 7, and 2021. Then add up the individual numbers as follows: $5 + 7 + 2 + 0 + 2 + 1 = 17$, which is the number of card XVII The Star. If your number is higher than 21, add the digits. Say it comes to 33—just add $3 + 3 = 6$, for VI The Lovers. So the idea is to add up the digits, and then, if necessary, add them again so you always arrive at a major arcana number.

Place your major arcana card before you, faceup. Next, ask the cards for guidance for the day ahead. Shuffle, choose one card (see page 15), and lay it by your major card.

Card for today

Advice

In this example, the Star represents hope, healing, and inspiration. With the Page of Cups as advice, the guidance is to be open to new ideas. You may benefit from the company of a young person or spending time doing what brings you joy and a sense of playfulness.

Looking at Future Dates

You can use the same technique to look at a date in the future, such as the date of a celebration, examination results, or vacation. Use the future date to calculate your major arcana card as above, then select a second card for guidance.

WEEK AHEAD

For a weekly forecast, shuffle your deck and take out one card, placing it facedown as the Significator for the reading (see page 15). This card gives you the general theme of the week, but interpret it last (otherwise it may influence how you interpret the cards for each day). Next, choose seven cards, placing them facedown. So, lay down cards 1, 2, and 3 with gaps between them, place card 4 (Sunday) at the end, again leaving a gap, then lay down cards 5, 6, and 7 to complete the week.

The layout comes from the orbit speed of the planet to which each day relates:

Monday: The Moon

Tuesday: Mars

Wednesday: Mercury

Thursday: Jupiter

Friday: Venus

Saturday: Saturn

Sunday: The Sun

The Greek scholar Ptolemy (90–168 CE) arranged the planets according to the speed of their orbits, beginning with the fastest moving, The Moon, followed by Mercury, Venus, The Sun, Mars, Jupiter, and finally, tardy Saturn. So, the cards are laid down according to Ptolemy's order—card 1 is Monday (The Moon), card 2 is Wednesday (Mercury), and so on.

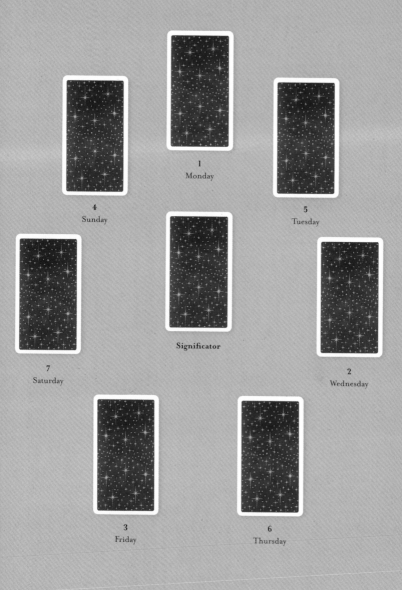

1
Monday

4
Sunday

5
Tuesday

Significator

7
Saturday

2
Wednesday

3
Friday

6
Thursday

MONTH AHEAD

This spread looks at the month in ten cards. There are two cards for each week, plus two for days of the month beyond 28. If you're reading for a February not in a leap year, you'll only need eight cards to represent its 28 days; a reading for any other month will follow the example below. The cards in the left-hand column reveal what's happening that week, while the cards to the right offer guidance.

Shuffle your cards, asking, "What do I need to know about the coming month?" Then choose and lay your cards facedown. Turn over cards 1 and 2 first and interpret them, then repeat. Make a note of your predictions and insights for each week as you go for future reference.

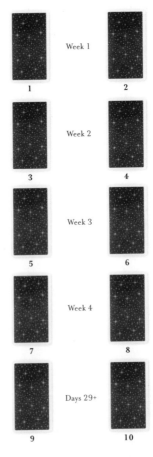

1	Week 1	**2**
3	Week 2	**4**
5	Week 3	**6**
7	Week 4	**8**
9	Days 29+	**10**

What's happening   Advice/action to take

Example reading: Here's an example for the month of July, which has 31 days.

Week 1

1

2

Week 2

3

4

Week 3

5

6

Week 4

7

8

Days
29–31

9

10

What's happening   Advice/action to take

The Reading in Brief

Cards 1 and 2:
The Seven of Cups and VII The Chariot. Everything feels up in the air; there are many possibilities. The advice is to be pragmatic—to be decisive and move forward.

Cards 3 and 4:
Four of Pentacles and Three of Cups. A stable situation. The advice is to celebrate and share rather than keep your good fortune to yourself.

Cards 5 and 6:
The Sun and the Nine of Wands. Growth and success; a happy place. The advice is to consider whether you need to lower or raise your boundaries.

Cards 7 and 8:
Queen of Swords and Eight of Coins. New demands on your time due to your ambition or the expectations of the queen in your life. The guidance here is that diligence will bring reward.

Cards 9 and 10:
Five of Wands and Three of Coins. You'll feel challenged, but it's worth enduring a test because you will create what you desire.

LUNAR MONTH

This simple spread, to be laid on a new moon, uses four cards to symbolize four key moon phases: the new moon for beginnings, the first quarter for decisions for future growth, the full moon for culmination and release, and the quiet third quarter for surrender and decrease.

You may find it helpful to photocopy the spread layout here and write in the upcoming dates for the next moon cycle, available from online lunar calendars.

Shuffle your cards, asking, "What can I create? What's emerging from the moon's shadow?" Then choose and lay out your cards as shown opposite.

Card 1: New moon. *What is beginning this lunar month.*

Card 2: First quarter. *Choices. Necessary decisions.*

Card 3: Full moon. *The likely outcome. What to reflect on.*

Card 4: Third quarter. *What to release to clear the way ahead.*

When interpreting your cards, see whether they complement the moon phase. For example, Four of Swords as card 3 in the third quarter means time out during a phase of declining energy, advising you to rest in tune with the moon's quiet decrease. A productive card such as one of the Aces or III The Empress as card 3 chimes with the new energy of the new moon. If some of your cards appear to contradict the lunar flow, you can use their guidance to move forward. For example, X The Wheel of Fortune as card 4 works well in the third quarter, because the Wheel asks you to surrender to fate; this card as card 2, however, could suggest you're relinquishing control when it's time to be making decisions.

1

4

2

3

YEAR AHEAD

This is a great reading for the beginning of the calendar year in January. Or you may have a time of year that feels like a new year to you. For example, this could be March, the beginning of the astrological new year with the sign of Aries, or Samhain (Halloween) for the Wiccan new year. And of course, you can practice this spread at any time by counting card 1 as the present month.

First, choose a Significator (see page 15) that most represents you, but don't remove it from the deck yet. You may prefer a Court card such as the Queen of Cups or King of Wands, or a major arcana card such as the Hermit, Emperor, Star, or High Priestess. With your Significator still in the deck, count 12 cards to the right of the Significator and place them facedown in the layout shown opposite, with the Significator faceup in the center. If you find your Significator toward the top of the deck, you'll need to continue counting cards from the bottom. The easiest way to do this is to spread out the cards in a fan shape, as shown below.

To interpret your cards, you may find it easier to group them by season— so read spring's three cards together, then summer's, fall's, and winter's. Appreciate how the cards connect or contrast with each other in terms of feel, symbol, element, or color. Note your interpretations as you go.

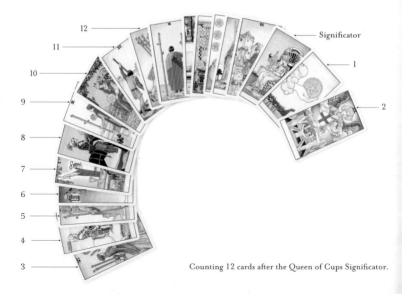

Counting 12 cards after the Queen of Cups Significator.

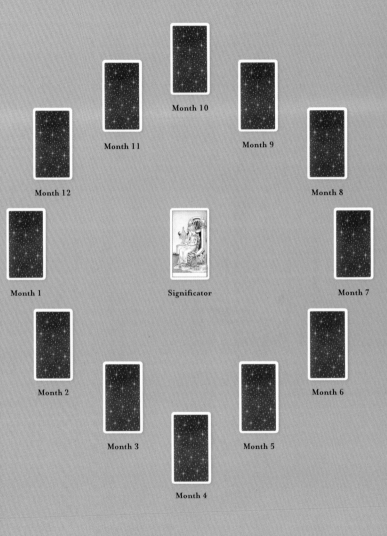

Month 10

Month 11

Month 12

Month 9

Month 8

Month 1

Significator

Month 7

Month 2

Month 6

Month 3

Month 5

Month 4

Using the Year Ahead as a Horoscope Spread

You can work with the Year Ahead spread as a horoscope for the upcoming year. Each card represents an astrological sign and an aspect of your life. So month 1 becomes Aries; month 2, Taurus; and so on. Each card position takes the following meaning:

Card 1, Aries: *Self-image*

Card 2, Taurus: *Money and resources*

Card 3, Gemini: *Communication and ideas*

Card 4, Cancer: *Home and family*

Card 5, Leo: *Creativity and self-expression*

Card 6, Virgo: *Work and well-being*

Card 7, Libra: *Relationships*

Card 8, Scorpio: *What is hidden or past*

Card 9, Sagittarius: *Knowledge, spirituality*

Card 10, Capricorn: *Career and ambition*

Card 11, Aquarius: *Community and support*

Card 12, Pisces: *Inner self, subconscious*

To lay your Year Ahead horoscope, shuffle the deck as you open up to the potential of the coming year. Lay the first card as your Significator (S), the theme for the coming year, followed by cards 1 to 12. Keep the Significator facedown and turn it faceup at the end of the reading, so it doesn't subtly influence your previous card interpretations.

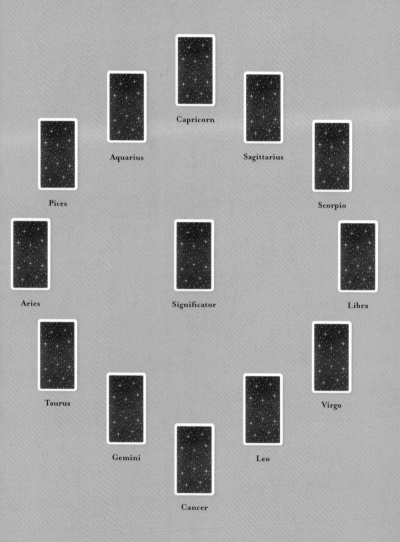

Capricorn

Aquarius   Sagittarius

Pices   Scorpio

Aries   Significator   Libra

Taurus   Virgo

Gemini   Leo

Cancer

Counting 12 cards after the Queen of Cups Significator.

TIMING USING THE MAJOR ARCANA CARDS

Each major arcana card relates to a planet or sign of the zodiac.
You can work with the zodiac signs to divine a timescale. For example,
V The Hierophant comes under the sign of Taurus, so the event in
question could happen during the time of Taurus (April 20 to May 20).
The cards with associated astrological signs are as below and follow the
Golden Dawn system (see pages 81 and 83).

CARD	SIGN	DATE
IV The Emperor	Aries	March 21–April 19
V The Hierophant	Taurus	April 20–May 20
VI The Lovers	Gemini	May 21–June 20
VII The Chariot	Cancer	June 21–July 22
VIII Strength	Leo	July 23–August 22
IX The Hermit	Virgo	August 23–September 22
XI Justice	Libra	September 23–October 22
XIII Death	Scorpio	October 23–November 21
XIV Temperance	Sagittarius	November 22–December 21
XV The Devil	Capricorn	December 22–January 20
XVII The Star	Aquarius	January 21–February 18
XVIII The Moon	Pisces	February 19–March 20

TIMING USING THE MINOR ARCANA CARDS IN THE FUTURE POSITION

You can use the card in the "future" position in a spread to predict an event. If it's a minor arcana card, the card's suit reveals days, weeks, months, or one year and beyond. If there is no minor arcana card in this position, lay down a card from the top of the deck until you find a numbered minor card, and place it alongside the future card. In this Past, Present, Future spread, we take card 3 for the future as our timing guide.

| 1 | 2 | 3 |
| Past | Present | Future |

The Six of Cups gives a prediction of six days. In the Celtic Cross (see pages 124 to 131) we take card 6, the near future, to give a timescale. Again, if this is not a minor number card, go through the deck as above to find one—but be sure to do this after you have laid out the other cards in the spread. The timing alignments for all the suits are as follows:

CUPS	WANDS	SWORDS	PENTACLES
Days	Weeks	Months	Years

There are also associations for suits and seasons:

CUPS	WANDS	SWORDS	PENTACLES
Winter	Spring	Summer	Fall

Although this system is a great starting point for timing in readings, it's clear that the Ten of Pentacles, for example, for ten years' time in fall, far exceeds the usual timescale of a reading (and it's highly unlikely we would want to see this far ahead, even if it were possible). An alternative approach is to work with numbers as symbols; symbols stimulate our intuition and open a door to further wisdom.

NUMBERS AS SYMBOLS

When giving timings in readings, numbers can lock us into fortune-telling mode, in which everything is defined, from "the advent of a tall, dark stranger" to "windfall in the month of June." Your approach to numbers may also be informed by how comfortable you were learning math at school. If you found math difficult, you may feel that numbers take you to the conscious, logical place in your mind—a space less conducive to the intuitive flow of tarot reading. But when you see numbers just like other symbols on your cards, more information comes to you as you read.

Technique 1: From Number to Calendar

Look at the numbered minor arcana card(s) that represents the future in your reading (if you don't have a numbered minor arcana card for the future, take the next one from the deck; see page 94).

Meditate on the number. See it as a shape, not a quantity. This helps release your association with numbers as finite characters and generates a feeling of flow and creativity. What might that number represent?

Take the number's shape into your third eye (the chakra, or energy point between your eyebrows). The third eye represents intuition and insight. Close your eyes and visualize your number symbol entering your third eye, lifting from the card and floating in. Close your eyes and continue to see the number symbol in your mind. Ask the number to show you what you need to know now.

A calendar of the year appears before you. You may see this as blocks of numbers—one block for each month together on a page—or, as I see it, as a circle divided into twelve segments. See what arises spontaneously; you will see time in a way that is unique to you. Perhaps it will be in the form of a diary, with the pages flipping forward or backward, then stopping at a particular month. Or maybe you will see the seasons like a slideshow.

What happens next is a strong pull toward one or more months of the year. In my circular calendar, significant months have darker segments, drawing my attention to them. The part of the month that is darkest represents the most significant time—toward the beginning, middle, or end of a month. You might see an important month differently. Perhaps June, on your mental calendar, is highlighted in pink. Or you may feel a subtle flip in your solar plexus when your imaginary diary flips to a certain page. Note that these impressions are often fleeting, and they need to be caught quickly; write them down or say them aloud during the reading. If we think too long about what we're experiencing, the detail begins to dissolve.

Technique 2: One Number Leads to Another

You may find that when you meditate on a number on any card, major or minor, you sense a different number coming through. It's as if the original number acts as a passkey, taking you through a doorway to a hidden number. If so, hold this new number in your mind and look again at the number on the card. Does this new number feel strong? If so, take it as your timescale. So if you gazed at the 7 on the Seven of Cups and got the number 11, you'd take 11 as your timescale number. You do not need to go further than this in a reading; you can give 11 as a significant number for timing and ask the person you are reading for to take note. They may interpret this for themselves in terms of days or weeks, or as the 11th month of the year, for example. The querent may also have their own association with the number 11, such as the date of an anniversary.

When you work with numbers as symbols, more information becomes available during the reading. You may be drawn to go back to a card in a spread and have more to say about the situation it represents. A reading isn't necessarily linear. We may read the cards in the order in which they are laid down but be called back to cards that symbolize particular situations or messages. Follow the flow and move around the spread as new insights arise. When you're guided by symbols, the traditional meanings of the cards fall away. You can be completely in the moment, allowing a number symbol— or any symbol on any card—to guide you through the reading. This is a very powerful technique because it helps you stay in the moment. You're not in the past, trying to remember what a card means; you're fully present, working with the symbols you see, which makes for a deeper, more engaged reading.

EXERCISE: FINDING MORE NUMBERS IN YOUR CARDS

With a number mindset, you'll find that you start seeing numbers in more places. Take out the Magician. His card number is I, but there's an infinity symbol (a sideways Eight, known as the lemniscate) above the crown of his head, for the eternal flow of energy. When this card appears in your reading, the lemniscate may draw you in; as Eight represents change and reward, the meaning of Eight can add another layer to your card interpretation.

Go through your deck and pull out all the cards that feature the infinity symbol. Examples include I The Magician, VIII Strength, Two of Pentacles, Nine of Cups, and XXI The World.

The Hidden Lemniscate

In early decks, the lamp of the Hermit, card IX, contained an hourglass, the shape of the lemniscate, rather than the star we see today (see page 104). The hourglass signified the Hermit's origins as Father Time and the Roman god Saturn (the Greek Cronus).

The lemniscate may also appear partially formed. In the Four of Cups, we see a downcast figure with arms crossed. One hand is tucked behind his sleeve, out of sight, symbolizing blocked energy: If he accepted the cup, life could flow again. Compare the figure on the Four of Cups (see page 104) to that of the Nine; we see how the unbroken lemniscate of the Nine symbolizes all the positives of this "wish card": Being part of the current, or eternal flow, of universal energy helps us manifest what we desire.

The lemniscate appears on the Magician, Strength, and Two of Pentacles, and is suggested by the crossed arms of the figure on the Nine of Cups. The red ribbon ties on the World's mandorla wreath also take the shape of the lemniscate.

THE HANGED MAN

The Hanged Man's Four

The Hanged Man's legs make the shape of the number 4 (turn the card upside down and you'll see 4 as a mirror image). When the card was first created, the 4 shape intentionally evoked the fylfot cross, an early Christian symbol. If we see Four as stability, this echoes the experience of the Hanged Man: He trusts his precarious position, knowing it will be for his higher good.

These examples are starting points, and I hope you find many more number forms in your cards—and that the number meanings enrich your readings.

THE HERMIT

4

NUMBER TECHNIQUES IN TAROT SPREADS

(

Tarot spreads—and there are hundreds of them—use a variety of numbers of cards, from a one-card daily reading to the extensive ten-card Celtic Cross. When you understand the energy of numbers, you can align the theme of your reading with your choice of spread.

When we come across tarot spreads, we're often drawn to the look and theme of the layout rather than the quantity of cards. Although it's natural to choose any spread that resonates with you, the quantity of cards you lay down has meaning, too: The number of cards in a spread creates a particular numeric energy that supports the purpose of your reading.

So, before you read, consider the number of cards in your chosen spread. For example, you could opt for a two-card reading to explore issues around partnership, or you could choose a five-card reading to get to the heart of a current challenge. In this way, you're aligning the quantity of cards with the nature of your situation.

BOOST THE ALIGNMENT

To further align your layout with your reading theme, read with the majors plus one minor arcana suit that reflects the nature of your question. For example, for a love reading, take out the suit of Cups and shuffle it into your majors. If you're looking into the outcome of a court case, shuffle just the suit of Swords into the majors. To divine the outcome of a trip or creative project, work with Wands; for home and money matters, choose Pentacles.

PAIRS READING FOR LOVE

Twos represent partnership and can also reveal the tension of opposites. This pairs reading explores the dynamics of a relationship and its future potential. One card represents you, and the other card signifies your current or potential partner.

From the Court cards (the Pages, Knights, Queens, and Kings) choose one card for you and one card to represent the person in question. You can choose any Court you like: Kings or Knights don't need to represent someone who identifies as male, for example. These two cards are known as Significators (see page 15) because they signify people and act as the focus for your love reading.

Then shuffle the rest of the deck, divide it into two piles, and place the piles facedown. One pile represents you, and the second pile represents the person in question. Take two cards from the first pile and place them in positions 1 and 3. Take cards 2 and 4 from the other pile and place them facedown.

When you're ready, turn cards 1 and 2 faceup and interpret them together. Repeat for cards 3 and 4. Next, shuffle the two piles of cards together to make one pile, as cards 5 and 6 will show the combined energy of your relationship.

Pairs for Love

You
(Significator)

The Other Person
(Significator)

5
*Hidden
challenges*

1
*What the relationship
means to you*

2
*What the relationship
means to them*

6
*Secret to a successful
relationship*

3
*What you bring to the
relationship*

4
*What they bring to the
relationship*

THREE-CARD READING FOR PREDICTION

Use three cards to investigate any situation that's dynamic and already in progress. This way, the symbolism of Three aligns with your subject, which further empowers your reading.

Three, the number of energy and creativity, represents the key elements of a story: beginning, middle, and end. In tarot, we have a three-card reading known as Past, Present, Future. Card 1 is for the past (the beginning), card 2 reveals the present circumstances (the middle part), and card 3 is for the future (the ending). *Prediction* here means the most likely outcome given the present influences.

Shuffle the whole deck and pose your question, such as "What's the likely outcome of [a given] situation?" Choose three cards (see page 15) and lay them as shown. You can interpret them one by one or turn over all three at once.

1
Past—the origins of
the present situation

2
Present—what's
happening now

3
Future—the most
likely outcome

MORE THREE-CARD SPREADS

You can also assign card positions that don't embrace a time line at all. For example, you might look at aspects of a relationship or creative venture. Here are some ideas:

Body, mind, spirit

Problem, challenges, advice

Relationship, how they feel, how you feel

Money, career, life purpose

Love, work, money

Positives, negatives, solution

Outer self, inner self, higher self

Ideas, focus, expression

FOUR-CARD READING FOR REFLECTION

Four is the number of stability. For this reason, four-card readings are perfect for personal reflection and insight; we can only reflect from a secure position, so the four in the number of cards reinforces the reading's purpose. Card 1 oversees the reading, offering a theme, while cards 2, 3, and 4 reveal current and upcoming issues. As this reading helps you contemplate the moment and current influences, it looks at the present and the near future, usually the next day or two.

As this is a spread just for you, it helps to speak it aloud as you go. This makes your reading come alive and helps you commit to your interpretations. Speaking aloud is particularly helpful if you tend to hesitate or overthink your cards; it acts as a circuit breaker, helping your reading flow.

Shuffle the whole deck and pose your question, such as "What do I need to become aware of today?" Choose your cards (see page 15) and lay them facedown in the order shown. Don't turn over card 1 yet, as you'll do this at the end. Turn over cards 2, 3, and 4, read them, and then look at card 1. You can revisit your interpretations in the light of card 1 and see how your cards connect.

Reflection Reading

1

Theme for you now and over
the next few days

2   3   4

Main issues for you now and over the next few days

FIVE-CARD READINGS FOR CHALLENGES AND TRUTH

Although all readings could be said to uncover truth, laying five cards symbolizes the challenge you're currently facing. Five is traditionally known as the number of mankind. With five cards, we get to see what is happening in the wider world and how people and external issues impact our lives. The meanings of the minor arcana Fives reveal the kind of situations we fear that drive us to find truth and meaning when we are tested. The Five of Swords signifies humiliation and ruin, the Five of Cups signifies sadness and grief due to loss, the Five of Wands is a test of strength and values, and the Five of Pentacles reveals fear of poverty and rejection. We naturally want to avert these scenarios, or at least understand why they might arise. However, do consider that the number Five is also associated with perfection and spiritual living (V The Hierophant interprets the word of God). So whatever challenge you face is an opportunity for spiritual growth.

The two spreads here each use five cards. The What's Going On? spread looks at an external influence and its likely impact, with an advice card (5) for guidance. The Cross of Truth makes you and your desires the focus. Choose the spread that best aligns with your situation.

Shuffle the whole deck, asking, "What's going on now with [a given person/situation]?" Then choose your cards (see page 15), laying them in the order shown in the spread you choose. Lay all the cards facedown, and then turn them faceup together and interpret them.

Tip: In the Cross of Truth, if you're concerned that seeing your outcome card will influence how you interpret the other cards, leave it facedown until you've finished reading the previous cards.

What's Going On?

1
Present situation

2
Progress—what's happening,
unknown to you

5
Growth—what you can
learn from this experience

4
What action this person is
likely to take, or how the
situation is likely to unfold

3
The deeper reason
for this situation

The Cross of Truth

5
The most likely outcome

4
What opposes or blocks
you—the disadvantages

2
What you want
or most desire

3
What supports you—
the advantages

1
Present situation

SIXES AND SEVENS:
CARD-COUNTING FOR FAST INSIGHT

Do you know the saying "I'm all at sixes and sevens"? It's an idiom that means feeling scattered, distracted, and confused. The number Six represents harmony, while Seven means risk, potential, and mysteries. So Six and Seven together express a state of unrest.

For this reading, we use a card-counting technique, which was used for fortune-telling before the concept of spreads and card positions. It's an instant way to read and uses the numbers Six and Seven—namely the sixth and seventh cards that come before and after the Two of Pentacles. The Two of Pentacles symbolizes choices and the tension that can arise during the decision-making process, but you can instead choose any other card that sums up how you're feeling.

What's intriguing about this reading is that you don't need a question. The cards appear to tell you exactly what you need to know, guiding you toward the decision that frees you from that sixes-and-sevens feeling.

Shuffle your deck. Then look through the cards faceup until you find the Two of Pentacles. Don't remove the card, as it stays where it is for the whole reading. Next, find the sixth and seventh cards that come before the Two of Pentacles and place them before you. Go back to your Two of Pentacles and this time count six and seven cards ahead of it. Remove those two cards as well. Interpret their meanings. Then regather the deck, hold it facedown, and draw the bottom card. This card is advice on what to do next.

Six and Seven for Insight

Past 6 and 7:
The reason for your present situation

Future 6 and 7:
What you need to know about the future

Bottom card in the deck:
Advice

Tip: If you find your Two of Pentacles near the very front or back of the deck, you'll need to continue counting around the deck. One way to do this is to spread the cards in a circle so the Two of Pentacles is at the top; then you can clearly see your cards and count your sixth and seventh cards to the left and right. If the Two of Pentacles is also your advice card, your issue needs more time to resolve. Repeat the reading in two days.

EIGHT-CARD READING FOR DECISIONS

Eight is the number of change, regeneration, and flowing energy. This spread helps you see what change you most need by laying cards for each option, so you can weigh the advantages and disadvantages. The final card for each option reveals the most likely outcome should you choose it.

Shuffle the whole deck, focusing on your first option. For example, this might be staying in your current role at work, spending money, trusting a new friend, or beginning a project. When you're ready, choose four cards (see page 15) and lay them from left to right under option 1. Then shuffle the remaining deck, this time asking about an alternative option you're considering, and lay four cards under option 2.

When you interpret your cards, you can easily compare the pros and cons of each path by looking at the cards with the same number.

Which Way Is Right for Me?

Option 1

1	2	3	4
How you feel about this option	Disadvantages or blocks	Advantages and strengths	Likely outcome if this option is chosen

Option 2

1	2	3	4
How you feel about this option	Disadvantages or blocks	Advantages and strengths	Likely outcome if this option is chosen

NINE-CARD READING FOR LIFE LESSONS

Nine comprises three threes. As three is a dynamic, creative number, the triple three symbolizes intensity before resolution. In tarot, Nine denotes holding on before moving on. It's the point at which we integrate our experiences and learn lessons.

Try this spread when you're on the cusp of the new—you may have a feeling of anticipation, having made some changes seen in the spread of Eight (see pages 120 to 121), and would like to see how these changes may play out in the future.

Shuffle the whole deck, asking what you need to know. For example, you might ask, "What lessons have I learned, or do I need to learn, before I can move forward?"

Choose nine cards (see page 15) and lay them facedown as shown. Now see the spread as three vertical columns and intuitively choose one card from each. Place these three cards below to make a row, still facedown. Then turn the cards faceup and interpret them.

To develop the reading, you can repeat the process two more times, so you have three rows of cards in total. The second row reveals your contribution in relationships and in society. The third reveals what you can receive.

Choose one card from each column to make a new row of cards to interpret.

Life Lessons

Example: You will see from the illustration that the three selected cards from the columns in this reading are XI Justice, the Ten of Pentacles, and the Four of Wands. In a love reading for Jenna, I saw that a key value for her was justice. In the past she'd been treated unfairly and had since focused on self-value. The Ten of Pentacles revealed a love commitment and sharing resources—Jenna had just begun a business with a new partner. The Four of Wands in the future expressed celebration, freedom, and happiness, a reward for a lesson learned.

Left-hand card:	Center card:	Right-hand card:
Important past event, lesson, or influence that affects you now	What's changing in your life at this moment	Future influences

TEN-CARD SPREADS FOR EVERYTHING

Ten is the number of completion and resolution. When you want a detailed answer to a question—or simply an overview of current influences—choose the ten-card Celtic Cross spread. Three versions of the cross are shown here, so you can choose the version you feel most drawn to.

The Celtic Cross presents the whole picture by bringing together ten cards that symbolize a host of internal and external influences. It looks at the past, the reason for the reading, your immediate concerns and challenges, your environment, how you're perceived, your hopes and fears, and the ultimate outcome. It's often the first spread professional readers use to get an overview of what's happening in a client's life, after which they focus in on one aspect of the spread and lay more cards for detail.

Shuffle the whole deck, asking your question. Choose your cards (see page 15) and lay them facedown in the sequence listed below and shown opposite. Interpret each card according to its position.

THE CELTIC CROSS (OPPOSITE)

1. Current circumstances

2. What is crossing or complementing you

3. The best you can expect at present

4. The hidden factors around you (this can also show the reason for the reading)

5. Past events influencing the present

6. Your next move

7. How you see yourself; what you can do

8. Your environment

9. Your hopes and fears

10. Outcome

The Celtic Cross

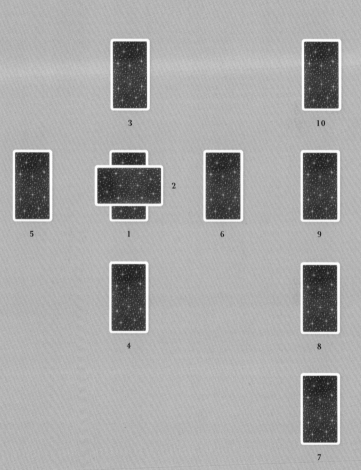

The Celtic Cross: Alternative Layout

Some readers lay cards 3, 4, and 5 in a different way, placing the cards clockwise as shown (see opposite). Cards 6 through 10 are the same as in the original spread.

THE CELTIC CROSS ALTERNATIVE LAYOUT (OPPOSITE)

1. Current circumstances

2. What is crossing or complementing you

3. The hidden factors around you (this can also show the reason for the reading)

4. Past events influencing the present

5. The best you can expect at present

6. Your next move

7. How you see yourself; what you can do

8. Your environment

9. Your hopes and fears

10. Outcome

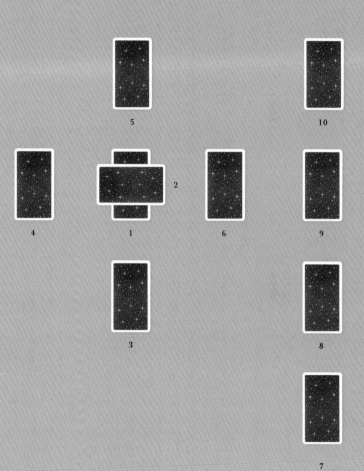

The Historical Cross: A. E. Waite

Occultist A. E. Waite (see pages 7 and 9) presented this spread, An Ancient Celtic Method of Divination, in his *The Pictorial Key to the Tarot* (1910).

Waite's Historical Cross uses ten cards plus a Significator.

Go through your cards faceup and choose your Significator, the card that best represents you or your situation. Place it faceup in the center. Then shuffle the remainder of the deck, asking your question. Choose your cards (see page 15). Place card 1 over the Significator, facedown, so the Significator is covered up. Say, "This covers me." Then place card 2 across card 1, saying, "This crosses me." Place card 3, saying, "This crowns me," and then card 4, saying, "This is beneath me." If you have a figure on your Significator card, see whether they're looking to your left. If so, you'll need to swap positions 5 and 6 so your figure is looking to the future. For any other card, go with the order of cards shown below. As you place card 5, say, "This is behind me," and for card 6, "This is before me."

WAITE'S CELTIC CROSS (OPPOSITE)

S. Significator—You/your situation.

1. What covers you. What is affecting you/your situation.

2. What crosses you. Obstacles. A positive card in this position means that there will not be serious obstacles.

3. What crowns you. The best that can be achieved in the present circumstances; your ideal outcome.

4. What is beneath you. The foundation of the matter. What has actually happened.

5. What is behind you. Past influence.

6. What is before you. Future influence.

7. Your position or attitude.

8. External influences—home, work, or friends, for example.

9. Your hopes or fears.

10. Outcome—the culmination of influences revealed in the preceding cards.

Waite's Celtic Cross

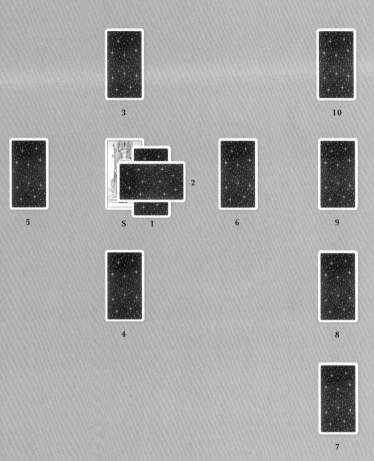

A figure on the Significator card always looks toward the future, card 6. If you had a Significator that looks to your left, the positions 5 and 6 swap: The left-hand card becomes the future and the right-hand card becomes the past.

FINDING THE QUINTESSENCE

The Quintessence is also known as the fifth element, the synthesis of the four elements of Air, Water, Fire and Earth. In a tarot reading, the Quintessence is a major arcana card that encapsulates the spirit of your reading. All you need do is add up the numbers on your cards in a spread and then reduce that number to 21 or less.

For the major arcana cards, use the number you see on the card. For the minor arcana, use the number on the card, designating Ace as 1. With Court cards, you can go two ways. Traditionally, they are disregarded, but some readers do assign numbers: Page as 11, Knight as 12, Queen as 13, and King as 14 (see page 82).

When you've decided how you want to assign numbers to your cards, it's time to add them. The example opposite, the Celtic Cross spread from page 82, shows you how to add up your cards in a spread. Here, Court cards are not counted.

If you used a Significator with your Celtic Cross (see page 15), add in the number for your Significator, too.

Finding a Second Quintessence

Each major arcana card has a reflection—one or two cards with which it shares a number link (see page 34). So, if your Quintessence is 8, for VIII Strength, you'll also see that 8 is the reduced number for card XVII The Star. Take out Strength and the Star and interpret them together to go deeper in your reading. Look for the similarities and differences. In this case, both show a maiden, but the Strength maiden is clothed and the Star maiden is naked. So there's an issue here about what we do publicly—a show of strength—and how we embrace our vulnerability. Strength has a single goal (managing a potential threat with grace), while the Star maiden is in a state of surrender. The message here is that soon it will be safe to let go.

The Quintessence in a Celtic Cross

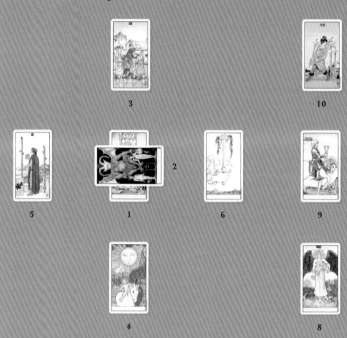

CARDS IN SPREAD		NUMBER
Card 1:	Queen of Swords	-
Card 2:	XV The Devil	15
Card 3:	Six of Cups	6
Card 4:	XIX The Sun	19
Card 5:	Two of Wands	2
Card 6:	Ace of Swords	1
Card 7:	Three of Pentacles	3
Card 8:	XIV Temperance	14
Card 9:	Knight of Cups	-
Card 10:	Seven of Swords	7
Total:		**67**

Add 6 + 7: 13 Quintessence card: XIII Death

The Quintessence card for the reading is Death, the card of transformation.

ADVANCED PRACTICE: MINORS TO MAJORS BY NUMBERS

As we saw in chapter 1 (pages 20 to 29), the major arcana cards can be grouped by number. Here, you'll learn how to group major and minor cards together by number or type and read them collectively. In readings, this means you can translate any minor card into a major in an instant.

The Minors to Majors process is one technique you can draw upon if you have some knowledge of the majors but feel overwhelmed when confronted by a minors-only spread. All you need do is pull out the majors connected with your minor cards—the list is below—and you'll get back into the flow.

You may already know that the Magician rules all the Aces, the Empress rules the Queens, and the Emperor rules the Kings. Here are my associations for all the minor arcana cards.

Minor Arcana Associations at a Glance

Aces . . . . The Fool, the Magician

Twos . . . . The Lovers

Threes . . . . Justice

Fours . . . . The Hanged Man

Fives . . . . The Devil

Sixes . . . . The World

Sevens . . . . Temperance

Eights . . . . Strength

Nines . . . . Wheel of Fortune

Tens . . . . Death

Pages. . . . . The Sun

Knights. . . . . The Chariot

Queens . . . . The Empress

Kings . . . . The Emperor

Tip: Note that in this system, not all major cards are linked with a group of minors; the High Priestess, Hierophant, Hermit, Tower, Star, Moon, and Judgment are not. However, you may choose to devise your own list that embraces these cards.

Aces: The Fool and the Magician

  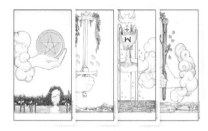

Aces as Ones stand for concepts and beginnings, which evoke both the Fool and the Magician. The Fool can be understood as an ideal (the idealistic youth, about to step into the world) and the Magician as action, through whom the idea takes form.

The Magician brings heaven down to earth to create magic. The four suits of the minor arcana—Swords, Cups, Wands, and Pentacles—are represented on the Magician's altar. The Magician harnesses the energy of the natural elements of all four suits to their will, engaging the mind (Swords), heart (Cups), body (Pentacles), and soul (Wands) to communicate and manifest their desire.

Twos and the Lovers: Turning Points

The Twos represent the choice aspect of the Lovers: the need for a mature decision. The figures on the Twos are largely static, suggesting the process of consideration over time, which may be procrastination (Swords), planning (Wands), flipping alternatives (Pentacles), or the long gaze into the eyes of the beloved (Cups). And of course, the Two of Cups evokes the literal love meaning of the Lovers in readings, and the Lovers in its composition, with the lion, symbol of passion and protection, echoing Archangel Raphael as the guiding force appearing above the couple.

Threes and Justice: Assessments

Looking at these dynamic Threes, we're cast into the role of observer or judge assessing a public activity. Three women dance in a garden (Cups); a craftsman holds court by a church (Pentacles); a journeyman atop a hill looks to the territory ahead (Wands); and the abstract heartbreak card (Swords) shows a rain-filled sky. We are drawn to wonder what the traveler is thinking as they scope out the landscape, or what the verdict on the craftsman's ideas will be after they step down from the bench. Even the Three of Cups' women might be celebrating the outcome of a trial or test.

Fours and the Hanged Man: Stasis and Retreat

The Fours express a fixed position, just like the Hanged Man, suspended in time yet content in his predicament. The dejected figure (Cups) is in retreat under a tree; the knight in repose might be a statue (Swords), while the wealthy merchant in the town square (Pentacles) might be a public statue. The spirited, joyful couple (Wands) have escaped to their ideal location, so this card expresses the bliss of the Hanged Man, symbolized by his halo and beatific smile. A further connection between the Fours and the Hanged Man is the 4 shape made by the Hanged Man's legs.

Fives and the Devil: Potential Pitfalls

The Fives show tests. How we manage these experiences leads either to the darkness of the Devil, the realm of conflict and restriction, or the garden of choice offered by the Lovers. This may be sorrow, disappointment, and bereavement (Cups); physical tests and tests of integrity (Wands); battle and humiliation (Swords); or the fear of isolation and poverty (Pentacles). We either lose ourselves or choose for ourselves. The Fives denote challenges that, if left untended, can lead us into temptation. In addition, the number 5 appears in the Devil's number, XV.

Sixes and the World: Microcosms of Completion

The Sixes are instances of completion, just as the World marks the completion of the major arcana cycle before we begin again with the Fool. The Sixes all illustrate a transaction, for example, giving money to the needy (Pentacles) or the gift of the cup and flower (Cups). Then we have the travelers (Swords) who can sail away, mission accomplished, presumably after paying for their passage, while the rider in the victory procession is rewarded with fame. The laurel wreath on the Six of Wands becomes the mandorla, or laurel garland, on the World.

Sevens and Temperance: The Struggle for Balance

Sevens are all about potential and how, with focus, we can still succeed if we put in time and effort. Temperance demonstrates the need for balance, patience, and ingenuity, whether a competitor is stealing from you (Swords) or you're tired of firefighting (Wands). Persist even when you think you've done enough (Pentacles) and don't delude yourself, head in the clouds (Cups). When Seven threatens to derail our dreams, Temperance, in the form of Archangel Michael, becomes a guiding light.

Eights and Strength: Grace Under Pressure

The Eights align naturally with Strength, the card of grace under pressure. We have work and dedication (Pentacles); the anxiety of entrapment (Swords); ever-expanding networks and communication (Wands); and, for the Eight of Cups' departing figure, the realization that something is missing. Fulfillment is elsewhere, and so the quest to find it must begin. Each scenario on the cards calls for strength: the strength to walk away (Cups), the strength to think our way out of the Eight of Swords' limiting mindset, the strength to strive for and achieve goals (Pentacles), or the strength to avoid overwhelm as the Eight of Wands speeds up the pace of life. We also see the number 8 in the lemniscate above the maiden's head.

Nines and the Wheel of Fortune: Intense Times

Nines are cards of accumulation and, therefore, intensity. Before the
completion of the Tens, we're realizing our gifts and burdens, from wish-
making and sharing (Cups) to enjoying luxuries (Pentacles). With the Nine
of Wands, we defend our past achievements (and wounds); or with the Nine
of Swords, we suffer discomfort and worry. As anxiety arises from having
no control over external situations, the Nine of Swords is a harbinger of
the Wheel of Fortune. The Wheel tells us what the Nine of Swords knew all
along: Control is an illusion. There are greater forces and cycles at work
over which we have little influence, so it's time to go with the flow.

Tens and Death: All the Endings

Tens for resolution link directly to Death, card of endings and change.
Whatever fullness amassed in the Nines now manifests: a sudden end
(Swords), complete fulfillment (Cups), consolidation and unification
(Pentacles), or impossible burdens (Wands). If positive, the lesson may
be to appreciate what we have and to continue to feed relationships and
creative projects with our energy. If negative, Death releases us from
outdated scenarios, relationships, and our own self-judgment. Overall,
the Tens and Death reveal an outcome that is ultimately true.

Pages and the Sun: Divine Children

Pages represent children and young people, which takes us to the Sun and its joyful child in a verdant garden. We might consider that the Page of Wands is the gardener (gardening as the work of the soul). The Page of Pentacles built the wall (the material world), the Page of Swords defends it, and the Page of Cups brings the Sun's warmth. In Jungian terms, the child of the Sun can be regarded as the archetype of the Divine Child; Jung says this archetype means "the completion of a long path." As card XIX in the major arcana sequence, the positioning of the Sun comes toward the end of the Fool's Journey (see pages 28 to 29) that the major arcana cycle represents.

Knights and the Chariot: Forging Ahead

The Knights are the four facets of the Chariot's rider. The Knight of Pentacles is the pragmatist, keeping the vehicle on the road. The Knight of Wands has the drive to initiate the journey; the Knight of Swords is the strategist, planning the route; and the Knight of Cups is the idealist, dreaming of distant lands. The purpose of the Chariot's journey might be revealed by the Knights, too, whether it is to find financial stability and work (Pentacles), a love quest (Cups), a battle (Swords), or adventure (Wands). In many readings, the Knight of Wands is the unfailing symbol of moving house—just as the Chariot departs the city, onward.

Queens and Kings: Aspects of the Empress and Emperor

The four Queens are personality aspects of the Mother archetype, the Empress: the empath (Cups); the nature-loving pragmatist (Pentacles); the dynamic creatrix and leader (Wands); and the independent thinker (Swords). There are also subtle visual connections between the cards. The Queen of Cups' plait echoes the Empress's laurel crown. The tassel on the Queen of Swords' bracelet is seen in the tassel on the Empress's bolster cushion. The Queen of Pentacles' roses appear on the Empress's dress, and the Queen of Wands' sunflower and wand are symbols of growth, just like the Empress's lush landscape.

Like the Queens, the four Kings work as four facets of the Emperor, symbol of order and structure. The King of Cups relates the Emperor's mastery of his emotions. The King of Swords is his intelligence and authority. The King of Pentacles represents establishment and power (and a willingness to do battle for his beliefs, as both this King and the Emperor wear armor). The King of Wands reveals the Emperor's spirit of adventure, charisma, and ability to communicate.

Note that Pages, Knights, Queens, and Kings can represent any person, and interpretations are not limited to the gender of the figure on the card. In addition, the Courts can represent situations (see chapter 2).

5

YOUR
BIRTH CARDS
AND TAROTSCOPE

B y using your date of birth, you can calculate your tarot birth cards, which reveal the influences that remain constant throughout your life. The tarotscope is an oracle based on your birth cards, showing the age at which your birth cards influence you the most, plus which other cards influence you, year by year.

TAROT BIRTH CARDS

Much like zodiac signs, your tarot birth cards reveal the influences around you from birth. They symbolize your life's themes—cycles and phases, lessons, challenges, and opportunities on your path. Everyone has two or three birth cards, and it's easy to find them by adding up the numbers in your date of birth. The number you arrive at relates to the number on a major arcana card.

For example, if your date of birth reduces to the number 6, you'd relate this to card 6 in the major arcana, VI The Lovers. Your second birth card will be XV The Devil, because the card's number, 15, also reduces to 6. In this way, you're using the record of your birth to find your birth cards—and discover truths about yourself through the tarot.

There are two ways to find your birth cards: by breaking down your date of birth to single digits and adding them up, or by adding up numbers in pairs.

Finding Your Birth Cards: Single Numbers

The first birth card is the highest major arcana card number you arrive at when adding up the digits in your date of birth. You do this by adding up the day, month, and year as follows.

For example, if your date of birth is March 16, 1981:
Add 3 (month) + 1 + 6 (day) + 1 + 9 + 8 + 1 (year) = 29

Because 29 is higher than the highest numbered major arcana card, which is 21, we reduce 29 by adding 2 + 9 = 11. So the first birth card is XI Justice. The second birth card is II The High Priestess, because 11 reduces to 2 (1 + 1 = 2). If your first birth card's number is a single digit, such as 4, you can't reduce it, but you can find your second birth card by working out which higher major arcana card reduces to four. In this case, it's XIII Death, because 13 reduces to 4 (see also the Birth Card Pairings list, on the opposite page).

Finding Your Birth Cards: The Pairs Method

The pairs method was devised by Ruth Ann and Wald Amberstone of the Tarot School, New York. To use the pairs method, add up the day and month as above, but split the year into two—so 1981, for example, becomes 19 and 81.

If your date of birth is March 16, 1981:
Add 3 (month) + 16 (day) + 19 (century) + 81 (year) = 119

Add the first two digits as a pair: 11 + 9 = 20. So the first birth card is XX Judgment. Then add up the digits again—20 as 2 + 0—and you have the second birth card, II The High Priestess.

Birth Card Pairings

The World and the Empress
Judgment and the High Priestess
The Sun, Wheel of Fortune, and the Magician
The Moon and the Hermit
The Star and Strength
The Tower and the Chariot
The Devil and the Lovers
Temperance and the Hierophant
Death and the Emperor
The Hanged Man and the Empress
Justice and the High Priestess

Birth-card pairing of Judgment and the High Priestess

Three Birth Cards

Most people have two birth cards, but as with any system, there is an anomaly: If your birth date reduces to 19, you will have three birth cards, which show three elements of your life's story.

Here's why. A reduced birth date of 19 relates to card XIX The Sun. Add together 19, 1 + 9 = 10, for the second birth card of X The Wheel of Fortune. But you can reduce this number again, 1 + 0 = 1, which gives I The Magician. So in the special instance of 19, you get to have three birth cards: XIX The Sun, X The Wheel of Fortune, and I The Magician.

For more on birth cards, see Appendix III: Further Reading for Ruth Ann and Wald Amberstone's online birth card calculator.

USING THE TAROTSCOPE

Your tarotscope presents the yearly influences of major arcana cards in 21-card cycles. Beginning with the birth cards for the first year of your life, your tarotscope shows you which pair of major arcana cards have been or will be influencing you during any given year in the past or future. This doesn't detract from the core influence of your birth cards; you can see your birth-card influences as fixed, like your zodiac sign, while the other pairs of cards in your tarotscope are like the shifting planets, bringing in new energies, challenges, and opportunities. Just find the page for your birth cards, look across at the age columns, and discover the cards that ruled that year of your life—and which cards will influence you in the present year and years to come.

The order of cards on the tarotscope pages relate to the pairs method for divining your birth cards. When you use the pairs method, your first birth card will usually be a higher number and your second card a lower number. That's why the tarotscope begins with The World and The Empress, then Judgment and the High Priestess, and so on.

Please note that the Fool is not included as a birth card and, therefore, it is not in the tarotscopes that follow. It's a 21-card cycle, rather than a 22-card cycle. Although the energy of the Fool is present in every card (and within us all), the Fool is seen as outside the major arcana sequence.

It's always interesting to take note of your "birth-card years" when your birth cards repeat (years 22, 43, 64, and 85). These years are often significant times in your life. And of course, you can choose any year and see how the cards ruling that period manifested for you. Birth cards are shown in bold, as below.

THE HANGED MAN AND THE EMPRESS NUMBERS 12/3

BIRTH CARDS		YOUR AGE				
Empress	**Hanged Man**	1	22	43	64	85
Emperor	Death	2	23	44	65	86
Hierophant	Temperance	3	24	45	66	87
Lovers	Devil	4	25	46	67	88
Chariot	Tower	5	26	47	68	89

Personalizing Your Tarotscope

This system is my own (which of course doesn't exclude the possibility that others have also devised this system, or a version of it, as spontaneously as I did). And in time, you may make your own associations and patterns. If, upon reading your tarotscope, you sense other cards were more dominant for you than those given for that year, pencil them in. For example, if you moved countries when you were 36 and saw this ending as the Death card, make a note on the page. Would the next card in the sequence, Temperance, be a fit for the following year? If so, keep going, as there may be an additional, hidden cycle of major arcana that also works for you.

THE WORLD AND THE EMPRESS
NUMBERS 21/3

BIRTH CARDS		YOUR AGE				
Empress	**World**	**1**	**22**	**43**	**64**	**85**
Emperor	Magician	2	23	44	65	86
Hierophant	High Priestess	3	24	45	66	87
Lovers	Empress	4	25	46	67	88
Chariot	Emperor	5	26	47	68	89
Strength	Hierophant	6	27	48	69	90
Hermit	Lovers	7	28	49	70	91
Wheel	Chariot	8	29	50	71	92
Justice	Strength	9	30	51	72	93
Hanged Man	Hermit	10	31	52	73	94
Death	Wheel	11	32	53	74	95
Temperance	Justice	12	33	54	75	96
Devil	Hanged Man	13	34	55	76	97
Tower	Death	14	35	56	77	98
Star	Temperance	15	36	57	78	99
Moon	Devil	16	37	58	79	100
Sun	Tower	17	38	59	80	
Judgment	Star	18	39	60	81	
World	Moon	19	40	61	82	
Magician	Sun	20	41	62	83	
High Priestess	Judgment	21	42	63	84	

JUDGMENT AND THE HIGH PRIESTESS
NUMBERS 20/2

BIRTH CARDS		YOUR AGE				
High Priestess	**Judgment**	**1**	**22**	**43**	**64**	**85**
Empress	World	2	23	44	65	86
Emperor	Magician	3	24	45	66	87
Hierophant	High Priestess	4	25	46	67	88
Lovers	Empress	5	26	47	68	89
Chariot	Emperor	6	27	48	69	90
Strength	Hierophant	7	28	49	70	91
Hermit	Lovers	8	29	50	71	92
Wheel	Chariot	9	30	51	72	93
Justice	Strength	10	31	52	73	94
Hanged Man	Hermit	11	32	53	74	95
Death	Wheel	12	33	54	75	96
Temperance	Justice	13	34	55	76	97
Devil	Hanged Man	14	35	56	77	98
Tower	Death	15	36	57	78	99
Star	Temperance	16	37	58	79	100
Moon	Devil	17	38	59	80	
Sun	Tower	18	39	60	81	
Judgment	Star	19	40	61	82	
World	Moon	20	41	62	83	
Magician	Sun	21	42	63	84	

THE SUN, WHEEL OF FORTUNE, AND MAGICIAN
NUMBERS 19/10/1

BIRTH CARDS		YOUR AGE					
Magician	**Wheel**	**Sun**	1	22	43	64	85
High Priestess	Justice	Judgment	2	23	44	65	86
Empress	Hanged Man	World	3	24	45	66	87
Emperor	Death	Magician	4	25	46	67	88
Hierophant	Temperance	High Priestess	5	26	47	68	89
Lovers	Devil	Empress	6	27	48	69	90
Chariot	Tower	Emperor	7	28	49	70	91
Strength	Star	Hierophant	8	29	50	71	92
Hermit	Moon	Lovers	9	30	51	72	93
Wheel	Sun	Chariot	10	31	52	73	94
Justice	Judgment	Strength	11	32	53	74	95
Hanged Man	World	Hermit	12	33	54	75	96
Death	Magician	Wheel	13	34	55	76	97
Temperance	High Priestess	Justice	14	35	56	77	98
Devil	Empress	Hanged Man	15	36	57	78	99
Tower	Emperor	Death	16	37	58	79	100
Star	Hierophant	Temperance	17	38	59	80	
Moon	Lovers	Devil	18	39	60	81	
Sun	Chariot	Tower	19	40	61	82	
Judgment	Strength	Star	20	41	62	83	
World	Hermit	Moon	21	42	63	84	

Note: If your birth date reduces to 19, the Sun, you have three birth cards: the Sun, Wheel of Fortune, and Magician. If your birth date reduces to 10, just read the Wheel and Magician rows.

THE MOON AND THE HERMIT
NUMBERS 18/9

BIRTH CARDS		YOUR AGE				
Hermit	**Moon**	**1**	**22**	**43**	**64**	**85**
Wheel	Sun	2	23	44	65	86
Justice	Judgment	3	24	45	66	87
Hanged Man	World	4	25	46	67	88
Death	Magician	5	26	47	68	89
Temperance	High Priestess	6	27	48	69	90
Devil	Empress	7	28	49	70	91
Tower	Emperor	8	29	50	71	92
Star	Hierophant	9	30	51	72	93
Moon	Lovers	10	31	52	73	94
Sun	Chariot	11	32	53	74	95
Judgment	Strength	12	33	54	75	96
World	Hermit	13	34	55	76	97
Magician	Wheel	14	35	56	77	98
High Priestess	Justice	15	36	57	78	99
Empress	Hanged Man	16	37	58	79	100
Emperor	Death	17	38	59	80	
Hierophant	Temperance	18	39	60	81	
Lovers	Devil	19	40	61	82	
Chariot	Tower	20	41	62	83	
Strength	Star	21	42	63	84	

THE STAR AND STRENGTH
NUMBERS 17/8

BIRTH CARDS		YOUR AGE				
Strength	**Star**	1	22	43	64	85
Hermit	Moon	2	23	44	65	86
Wheel	Sun	3	24	45	66	87
Justice	Judgment	4	25	46	67	88
Hanged Man	World	5	26	47	68	89
Death	Magician	6	27	48	69	90
Temperance	High Priestess	7	28	49	70	91
Devil	Empress	8	29	50	71	92
Tower	Emperor	9	30	51	72	93
Star	Hierophant	10	31	52	73	94
Moon	Lovers	11	32	53	74	95
Sun	Chariot	12	33	54	75	96
Judgment	Strength	13	34	55	76	97
World	Hermit	14	35	56	77	98
Magician	Wheel	15	36	57	78	99
High Priestess	Justice	16	37	58	79	100
Empress	Hanged Man	17	38	59	80	
Emperor	Death	18	39	60	81	
Hierophant	Temperance	19	40	61	82	
Lovers	Devil	20	41	62	83	
Chariot	Tower	21	42	63	84	

THE TOWER AND THE CHARIOT
NUMBERS 16/7

BIRTH CARDS		YOUR AGE				
Chariot	**Tower**	**1**	**22**	**43**	**64**	**85**
Strength	Star	2	23	44	65	86
Hermit	Moon	3	24	45	66	87
Wheel	Sun	4	25	46	67	88
Justice	Judgment	5	26	47	68	89
Hanged Man	World	6	27	48	69	90
Death	Magician	7	28	49	70	91
Temperance	High Priestess	8	29	50	71	92
Devil	Empress	9	30	51	72	93
Tower	Emperor	10	31	52	73	94
Star	Hierophant	11	32	53	74	95
Moon	Lovers	12	33	54	75	96
Sun	Chariot	13	34	55	76	97
Judgment	Strength	14	35	56	77	98
World	Hermit	15	36	57	78	99
Magician	Wheel	16	37	58	79	100
High Priestess	Justice	17	38	59	80	
Empress	Hanged Man	18	39	60	81	
Emperor	Death	19	40	61	82	
Hierophant	Temperance	20	41	62	83	
Lovers	Devil	21	42	63	84	

THE DEVIL AND THE LOVERS
NUMBERS 15/6

BIRTH CARDS		YOUR AGE				
Lovers	**Devil**	1	22	43	64	85
Chariot	Tower	2	23	44	65	86
Strength	Star	3	24	45	66	87
Hermit	Moon	4	25	46	67	88
Wheel	Sun	5	26	47	68	89
Justice	Judgment	6	27	48	69	90
Hanged Man	World	7	28	49	70	91
Death	Magician	8	29	50	71	92
Temperance	High Priestess	9	30	51	72	93
Devil	Empress	10	31	52	73	94
Tower	Emperor	11	32	53	74	95
Star	Hierophant	12	33	54	75	96
Moon	Lovers	13	34	55	76	97
Sun	Chariot	14	35	56	77	98
Judgment	Strength	15	36	57	78	99
World	Hermit	16	37	58	79	100
Magician	Wheel	17	38	59	80	
High Priestess	Justice	18	39	60	81	
Empress	Hanged Man	19	40	61	82	
Emperor	Death	20	41	62	83	
Hierophant	Temperance	21	42	63	84	

TEMPERANCE AND THE HIEROPHANT
NUMBERS 14/5

BIRTH CARDS		YOUR AGE				
Hierophant	**Temperance**	**1**	**22**	**43**	**64**	**85**
Lovers	Devil	2	23	44	65	86
Chariot	Tower	3	24	45	66	87
Strength	Star	4	25	46	67	88
Hermit	Moon	5	26	47	68	89
Wheel	Sun	6	27	48	69	90
Justice	Judgment	7	28	49	70	91
Hanged Man	World	8	29	50	71	92
Death	Magician	9	30	51	72	93
Temperance	High Priestess	10	31	52	73	94
Devil	Empress	11	32	53	74	95
Tower	Emperor	12	33	54	75	96
Star	Hierophant	13	34	55	76	97
Moon	Lovers	14	35	56	77	98
Sun	Chariot	15	36	57	78	99
Judgment	Strength	16	37	58	79	100
World	Hermit	17	38	59	80	
Magician	Wheel	18	39	60	81	
High Priestess	Justice	19	40	61	82	
Empress	Hanged Man	20	41	62	83	
Emperor	Death	21	42	63	84	

DEATH AND THE EMPEROR
NUMBERS 13/4

BIRTH CARDS		YOUR AGE				
Emperor	**Death**	1	22	43	64	85
Hierophant	Temperance	2	23	44	65	86
Lovers	Devil	3	24	45	66	87
Chariot	Tower	4	25	46	67	88
Strength	Star	5	26	47	68	89
Hermit	Moon	6	27	48	69	90
Wheel	Sun	7	28	49	70	91
Justice	Judgment	8	29	50	71	92
Hanged Man	World	9	30	51	72	93
Death	Magician	10	31	52	73	94
Temperance	High Priestess	11	32	53	74	95
Devil	Empress	12	33	54	75	96
Tower	Emperor	13	34	55	76	97
Star	Hierophant	14	35	56	77	98
Moon	Lovers	15	36	57	78	99
Sun	Chariot	16	37	58	79	100
Judgment	Strength	17	38	59	80	
World	Hermit	18	39	60	81	
Magician	Wheel	19	40	61	82	
High Priestess	Justice	20	41	62	83	
Empress	Hanged Man	21	42	63	84	

THE HANGED MAN AND THE EMPRESS
NUMBERS 12/3

BIRTH CARDS		YOUR AGE				
Empress	**Hanged Man**	**1**	**22**	**43**	**64**	**85**
Emperor	Death	2	23	44	65	86
Hierophant	Temperance	3	24	45	66	87
Lovers	Devil	4	25	46	67	88
Chariot	Tower	5	26	47	68	89
Strength	Star	6	27	48	69	90
Hermit	Moon	7	28	49	70	91
Wheel	Sun	8	29	50	71	92
Justice	Judgment	9	30	51	72	93
Hanged Man	World	10	31	52	73	94
Death	Magician	11	32	53	74	95
Temperance	High Priestess	12	33	54	75	96
Devil	Empress	13	34	55	76	97
Tower	Emperor	14	35	56	77	98
Star	Hierophant	15	36	57	78	99
Moon	Lovers	16	37	58	79	100
Sun	Chariot	17	38	59	80	
Judgment	Strength	18	39	60	81	
World	Hermit	19	40	61	82	
Magician	Wheel	20	41	62	83	
High Priestess	Justice	21	42	63	84	

JUSTICE AND THE HIGH PRIESTESS
NUMBERS 11/2

BIRTH CARDS		YOUR AGE				
High Priestess	**Justice**	1	22	43	64	85
Empress	Hanged Man	2	23	44	65	86
Emperor	Death	3	24	45	66	87
Hierophant	Temperance	4	25	46	67	88
Lovers	Devil	5	26	47	68	89
Chariot	Tower	6	27	48	69	90
Strength	Star	7	28	49	70	91
Hermit	Moon	8	29	50	71	92
Wheel	Sun	9	30	51	72	93
Justice	Judgment	10	31	52	73	94
Hanged Man	World	11	32	53	74	95
Death	Magician	12	33	54	75	96
Temperance	High Priestess	13	34	55	76	97
Devil	Empress	14	35	56	77	98
Tower	Emperor	15	36	57	78	99
Star	Hierophant	16	37	58	79	100
Moon	Lovers	17	38	59	80	
Sun	Chariot	18	39	60	81	
Judgment	Strength	19	40	61	82	
World	Hermit	20	41	62	83	
Magician	Wheel	21	42	63	84	

APPENDIX I:
TAROT AND KABBALAH

The Holy Kabbalah (Qabala, Cabala) is a mystical belief system derived from Judaism. Tarot, as it has evolved, has been deeply influenced by Kabbalist numerology and its central symbol known as the Tree of Life.

The Tree of Life Pathways and the Major Arcana

The twenty-two cards of the tarot's major arcana can be aligned with the twenty-two letters of the Hebrew alphabet, which in turn relate to the twenty-two pathways on the Tree of Life. Each letter of the alphabet is a sacred symbol, and the letter's shape is a clue to its meaning. For example, the letter Kaph is written as a sideways U, which symbolizes the palm of the hand or cup. (Kaph is one of seven "double" letters of the alphabet that express dualities such as life and death or peace and war.) Kaph's "palm" describes the concept of wealth and poverty. Kaph aligns with card X The Wheel of Fortune, the card of fate. Interpreting the card in the light of its Hebrew letter, we can see that the card expresses Kaph; the top of the Wheel brings a handful of money, whereas the Wheel's downturn, for loss, is the empty palm.

To work with the Tree of Life, look up a major arcana card on the tree using the list on the next page (to find a card's pathway, simply add 1 to the card's number). Then consider the card's associated Hebrew letter and symbol. Note that the double letters—Beth, Gimel, Daleth, Kaph, Peh, Resh, and Tau—also include qualities.

Divination with Sacred Letter-Symbols

The symbol associated with a card can operate on many levels. One way to work with the symbol is to visualize it and see what internal images and feelings arise. You may have instant associations for some. "Back of the head" for XVIII The Moon, for example, may give you words such as *hidden*, *unseen*, or *behind*, which align with the card's meaning of mysteries and the past. Other symbols may have a physical association; "enclosure" for VII The Chariot may recall, for you, the chariot on the card. "Hand" for the Hermit symbolizes the ten digits of the hand and the Hermit's pathway number. Hand also suggests counting to ten, or processing before reacting, which aligns with the Hermit's meaning of time and patience. A further meaning could be that our future is in our own hands—hence the Hermit as the solitary seeker of their soul's path.

MAJOR ARCANA CARD	TREE OF LIFE PATHWAY	HEBREW LETTER	SYMBOL
0 The Fool	1	A (Aleph)	Ox
I The Magician	2	B (Beth, Beit)	House
II The High Priestess	3	G (Gimel)	Camel
III The Empress	4	D (Daleth)	Door
IV The Emperor	5	H (Hei)	Window
V The Hierophant	6	U, V (Vau)	Nail, connector
VI The Lovers	7	Z (Zain)	Sword
VII The Chariot	8	Ch (Heth)	Fence, enclosure
VIII Strength	9	T (Teth)	Serpent
IX The Hermit	10	I, Y (Yod)	Hand
X The Wheel of Fortune	11	K (Kaph)	Palm, cup
XI Justice	12	L (Lamed)	Whip
XII The Hanged Man	13	M (Mem)	Water, oceans
XIII Death	14	N (Nun)	Fish
XIV Temperance	15	S (Samekh)	Support, crutch
XV The Devil	16	0 (Ayin)	Eye
XVI The Tower	17	P (Peh	Mouth
XVII The Star	18	Tz (Tzaddi)	Fish hook
XVIII The Moon	19	Q (Qoph)	Back of head
XIX The Sun	20	R (Resh)	Front of head, face
XX Judgment	21	Sh (Shin)	Tooth
XXI The World	22	Th (Tau)	Cross

QUALITY

Life/Death

Peace/War

Wisdom/Folly

Wealth/Poverty

Grace/Indignation

Fertility/Solitude

Power/Servitude

Traditionally, the numbering of the pathways runs from 1 to 32 rather than 1 to 22; the system used here is adapted for tarot study. There are also further meanings for the letters, including directions, body parts, and zodiac signs (see page 98). Consider the sephiroth that the pathways connect. The sephiroth, which are illustrated as spheres, are seen as emanations through which God created the world.

For example, 0 The Fool is on pathway 1, which links the sephirah of Kether and Chockmah. Kether's meaning is "divine light," and Chockmah relates to wisdom. A simple interpretation, therefore, is that the Fool is newly born (divine light) and on a path to self-knowledge and spiritual wisdom. Look at the pathway 12 for XI Justice; it connects Geburah, for power and judgment, with 6, Tiphareth, for beauty and rebirth. This encapsulates the experience of justice in that Geburah reveals the situation (justice; being judged) and Tiphareth reveals the highest outcome (beauty and rebirth).

1   Kether, the Crown: Divine light. Manifestation.

2   Chockmah, wisdom: Duality, opposites.

3   Binah, understanding: Expansion. Kindness.

4   Chesed (Hesed), grace and mercy: Love for all; peace, order.

5   Geburah, power: Judgment, force, necessity.

6   Tiphareth, beauty: Rebirth, harmony.

7   Netzach, endurance: Instinct, impulse, desire.

8   Hod, splendor: The conscious mind. Strategy. Cycles and phases.

9   Yesod, foundation: The unconscious mind. Hidden forces, change, transition.

10   Malkuth, the Kingdom: The physical world. Fulfillment.

THE TREE OF LIFE SEPHIROTH AND THE MINOR ARCANA

Aces:	1	Kether	Sixes:	6	Tiphareth
Twos:	2	Chockmah	Sevens:	7	Netzach
Threes:	3	Binah	Eights:	8	Hod
Fours:	4	Chesed	Nines:	9	Yesod
Fives:	5	Geburah	Tens:	10	Malkuth

To divine your own meanings for the minor arcana using the sephiroth, consider the suit and element of your card. For example, consider the Two of Swords. Twos fall under Chockmah, sephirah of wisdom, duality, and opposites. As the Two shows a figure with two crossed swords, there is inner conflict, as Swords take the suit of Air and the mind. What wisdom do we gain by working through choices that have become paralyzing? What can we learn about ourselves by confronting oppositional forces?

KABBALA: THE TREE OF LIFE PATHWAYS AND THE MAJOR ARCANA

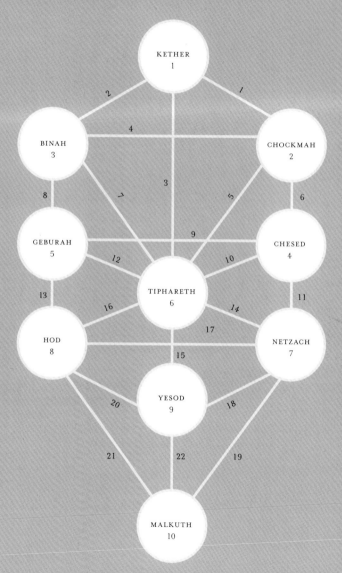

Comprising twenty-two pathways and ten sephiroth, the Tree of Life is both a map of creation and a map of our relationship with the universe; each sephirah (singular of *sephiroth*) represents a level of consciousness on our life's journey.

APPENDIX II:
DIRECTORY OF CARD MEANINGS

The Major Arcana

0
The Fool

Upright Meaning: Faith, risk, dreams, adventure. A new path or opportunity. Becoming a beginner.

Reversed Meaning: Idealism; impulsiveness. A need to plan.

I
The Magician

Upright Meaning: Action, creativity, initiation; making magic happen. Communication, travel, good news.

Reversed Meaning: Being misled; false appearances. Creative blocks, delay.

II
The High Priestess

Upright Meaning: Intuition, spirituality, secrets, discretion, wisdom. The card of the psychic and/or mentor.

Reversed Meaning: The wrong teacher or direction. Poor advice.

III
The Empress

Upright Meaning: Creativity, abundance, fertility, motherhood, nurturing. Personal and financial growth. Can represent a romantic partner.

Reversed Meaning: Financial strife, disruption; fertility/creativity issues.

IV
The Emperor

Upright Meaning: Ambition, structure, boundaries, tradition, fatherhood. A return to order after upheaval. Can represent a romantic partner.

Reversed Meaning: Bullying, stubbornness, incompetence.

V
The Hierophant

Upright Meaning: A step up. Education, personal development, self-togetherness/unity. Also, marriage.

Reversed Meaning: Abuse of power; issues with authority figures.

VI **The Lovers**	*Upright Meaning:* Love and choices; committing to a relationship. More broadly, long-term decisions.
	Reversed Meaning: Poor choices; inequality. Disappointment in a relationship.
VII **The Chariot**	*Upright Meaning:* Progress, determination, journeys. New energy and drive; the need for balance along the way. Also, new vehicles.
	Reversed Meaning: Delay to projects or travel plans. Also, egotism.
VIII **Strength**	*Upright Meaning:* Patience, endurance; grace under pressure. Also, wellness and good health.
	Reversed Meaning: Avoiding necessary conflict. Feeling ground down.
IX **The Hermit**	*Upright Meaning:* Reflection, productive solitude, wisdom (particularly esoteric knowledge). Also, healing after trauma; a quest for peace.
	Reversed Meaning: Loneliness; forced solitude.
X **The Wheel** **of Fortune**	*Upright Meaning:* Good luck; a positive, expansive phase. Past problems solved. Also a symbol for psychic work.
	Reversed Meaning: A run of bad luck is ending.
XI **Justice**	*Upright Meaning:* Legal matters. A decision goes in your favor (providing you have acted fairly). More broadly, balance restored.
	Reversed Meaning: A miscarriage of justice; unfairness.
XII **The Hanged Man**	*Upright Meaning:* Waiting, limbo; a delay offers a new perspective on a situation. Necessary compromises.
	Reversed Meaning: Naivete, avoidance. Living in the past.

XIII **Death**	*Upright Meaning:* Endings, change; clearing the way for beginnings. At an inner level, the death of the old self. *Reversed Meaning:* A refusal to let go. Resisting change.
XIV **Temperance**	*Upright Meaning:* Alchemy. Finding the right formula for maintaining balance. The need for careful management of resources. Working for the higher good. *Reversed Meaning:* Pressure due to others' demands. Conflicts of interest.
XV **The Devil**	*Upright Meaning:* Restriction, addiction, lust, affairs. Agreements that do not serve you; feeling controlled. *Reversed Meaning:* Guilt, obsession, weakness.
XVI **The Tower**	*Upright Meaning:* Breakdown, loss, illumination, truth. Forces beyond our control. Destruction as an opportunity to rebuild. *Reversed Meaning:* Inability to process trauma without blaming the self or others.
XVII **The Star**	*Upright Meaning:* Hope, inspiration, creativity, spiritual guidance. Courage in vulnerability. Also, a symbol of healing and of the healer. *Reversed Meaning:* False security; feeling lost.
XVIII **The Moon**	*Upright Meaning:* Doubt, deep questions, intuitive wisdom. Dreams, psychic work. *Reversed Meaning:* Buried emotions. Alternatively, the end of a phase of self-inquiry.
XIX **The Sun**	*Upright Meaning:* Optimism, happiness, relaxation; holidays. Removes any negative meanings in cards close to it in a spread. *Reversed Meaning:* Possible delays to plans, but otherwise positive.

XX Judgment	*Upright Meaning:* Memories, reviewing past actions; second chances, renewal. Also, mediumship.
	Reversed Meaning: Indecision, regret. Feeling stuck in old patterns.
XXI The World	*Upright Meaning:* Success, completion, rewards, celebration. Expansion, travel, new horizons.
	Reversed Meaning: As above, but with a degree of delay.

The Minor Arcana

The Suit of Cups

Element: Water, for the heart—relationships, love, sensitivity, imagination.

Ace of Cups	*Upright Meaning:* Love, passion, fertility, pregnancy; beginnings.
	Reversed Meaning: A false start. Emotional overload.
Two of Cups	*Upright Meaning:* Happy partnerships, soul mates, reconciliation, peace.
	Reversed Meaning: A partnership in trouble; potential trust issues.
Three of Cups	*Upright Meaning:* Celebration, parties, friendship; creativity, birth.
	Reversed Meaning: Emotional distance.
Four of Cups	*Upright Meaning:* Boredom; self-protection; need for inspiration.
	Reversed Meaning: Stubbornness, a closed mind.
Five of Cups	*Upright Meaning:* Loss and sadness; a need to look forward.
	Reversed Meaning: Recovery; the ending of a testing phase.
Six of Cups	*Upright Meaning:* A visitor; happy memories, friendship.
	Reversed Meaning: Living in the past.

Seven of Cups	*Upright Meaning:* Unrealized possibilities. Imagination, fantasy, mysticism.
	Reversed Meaning: Possible deception. Need for evidence or information.
Eight of Cups	*Upright Meaning:* Change; a natural ending. Also, travel.
	Reversed Meaning: Poor timing; feeling left behind.
Nine of Cups	*Upright Meaning:* A wish come true. Also, generosity, abundance, success.
	Reversed Meaning: Trying too hard. Also, narcissism.
Ten of Cups	*Upright Meaning:* Joy, family bonds; children's success; prosperity, a new home.
	Reversed Meaning: As above, with minor disruption/irritation.
Page of Cups	*Upright Meaning:* Socializing, feeling young at heart; love, artistic projects. As a person, an imaginative child or youth.
	Reversed Meaning: Delay to social plans. Immaturity; overindulgence.
Knight of Cups	*Upright Meaning:* An invitation. A proposal, a romance; new friends. As a person, a dreamy idealist.
	Reversed Meaning: Commitment issues. Empty promises.
Queen of Cups	*Upright Meaning:* Kindness, love, sensitivity, heart-centeredness. As a person, an intuitive. A romantic partner and/or the mother.
	Reversed Meaning: Unreasonable pressure. Financial glitches.
King of Cups	*Upright Meaning:* Love, generosity, support. As a person, a charismatic individual in touch with their emotions; a romantic partner and/or the father.
	Reversed Meaning: Avoiding emotional challenges.

The Suit of Pentacles

Element: Earth, for the body and physical realm—money, property, and possessions.

Ace of Pentacles	*Upright Meaning:* Money, success, beginnings; a new home or job.
	Reversed Meaning: Delay; money withheld. Materialism.
Two of Pentacles	*Upright Meaning:* Decisions; cash flow; often, choosing a location, job, or course.
	Reversed Meaning: Avoiding finances. Errors.
Three of Pentacles	*Upright Meaning:* Rewarding work; appreciation; property matters.
	Reversed Meaning: Commitment issues.
Four of Pentacles	*Upright Meaning:* Order and stability. Also, holding on to money tightly.
	Reversed Meaning: Materialism; problems with property.
Five of Pentacles	*Upright Meaning:* Fear of poverty and/or social isolation.
	Reversed Meaning: Poverty consciousness; suffering.
Six of Pentacles	*Upright Meaning:* Generosity; gifts given or received.
	Reversed Meaning: An offer with unreasonable conditions; a loan unpaid.
Seven of Pentacles	*Upright Meaning:* Success through consistent work.
	Reversed Meaning: Giving up too soon; doubting a goal.
Eight of Pentacles	*Upright Meaning:* Money and recognition. Exam success.
	Reversed Meaning: Lack of appreciation; unfulfilling work.
Nine of Pentacles	*Upright Meaning:* Comfort and home; stability and happiness.
	Reversed Meaning: Overspending. Lack of balance.

Ten of Pentacles	*Upright Meaning:* Love; a prosperous marriage; a new or second home. *Reversed Meaning:* Miscommunication. Conflict about money.
Page of Pentacles	*Upright Meaning:* New opportunities; travel, education, new work. As a person, a child or youth's well-earned success. *Reversed Meaning:* Problems or delays regarding finances or property.
Knight of Pentacles	*Upright Meaning:* Caution, devotion. Wise investments; work brings financial security. As a person, a loyal, dependable individual. *Reversed Meaning:* Stuckness. Poor financial advice.
Queen of Pentacles	*Upright Meaning:* Wealth, affection, care, love of nature. As a person, a generous woman who offers practical help. *Reversed Meaning:* Financial problems; debt. A lack of empathy.
King of Pentacles	*Upright Meaning:* Prosperity, protection. As a person, a generous, loyal individual who is supportive of others. *Reversed Meaning:* A lack of trust; greed.

The Suit of Swords

Element: Air, for the mind—decisions, challenges, and conflict.

Ace of Swords	*Upright Meaning:* Clarity. A breakthrough; success. *Reversed Meaning:* An unwelcome outcome. Potentially, trust issues.
Two of Swords	*Upright Meaning:* A truce or interlude; a pause before a decision. *Reversed Meaning:* Avoidance, procrastination.

Three of Swords *Upright Meaning:* Sorrow, stress, betrayal, disloyalty; seeing the truth.

Reversed Meaning: Acceptance, healing.

Four of Swords *Upright Meaning:* Time out. Also, recovery after illness or anxiety.

Reversed Meaning: A need to make peace with the present situation.

Five of Swords *Upright Meaning:* Loss, stressful conflict; the need to back down.

Reversed Meaning: Bullying; feeling coerced.

Six of Swords *Upright Meaning:* Finding peace after strife. Also, journeys.

Reversed Meaning: As above, but a slower process; journey delays.

Seven of Swords *Upright Meaning:* Theft, legal problems; need for protection and ingenuity.

Reversed Meaning: Victimhood. Need for courage and advice.

Eight of Swords *Upright Meaning:* Restriction; negative perception.

Reversed Meaning: As above, with strong emotion: guilt, shame.

Nine of Swords *Upright Meaning:* Anxiety, overthinking, insomnia.

Reversed Meaning: Feeling vulnerable or alone.

Ten of Swords *Upright Meaning:* A sudden and definitive ending.

Reversed Meaning: As above, with a heightened emotional reaction.

Page of Swords *Upright Meaning:* Vigilance. Details, paperwork; information. As a person, a child or youth who is ambitious and precise.

Reversed Meaning: Being misled; gossip.

Knight of Swords	*Upright Meaning:* Opposition, disputes. As a person, a driven individual who craves stimulation.
	Reversed Meaning: Drama; recklessness.
Queen of Swords	*Upright Meaning:* Instinct, intelligence. As a person, an independent woman, often a business leader; a single woman, a single parent.
	Reversed Meaning: Unreasonable behavior.
King of Swords	*Upright Meaning:* Decisions; legal issues, logic. As a person, a decision-maker who needs to assert their authority.
	Reversed Meaning: Coldness, oppression.

The Suit of Wands

Element: Fire, for the soul—passion, desire, communication.

Ace of Wands	*Upright Meaning:* Good news; inspiration, creativity, travel. Also, fertility.
	Reversed Meaning: Delay, miscommunication, fertility issues.
Two of Wands	*Upright Meaning:* Plans, partnership, positive influences.
	Reversed Meaning: Lack of commitment. Setbacks.
Three of Wands	*Upright Meaning:* Success, discovery, travel, happiness.
	Reversed Meaning: Delay, frustration.
Four of Wands	*Upright Meaning:* Freedom, love, harmony, celebration, holidays.
	Reversed Meaning: As above, with minor irritation or delay.
Five of Wands	*Upright Meaning:* Tests and competitions; the need to be heard.
	Reversed Meaning: Exaggeration, ego.

Six of Wands　*Upright Meaning:* The victory card: good news, deserved success, acknowledgment.

Reversed Meaning: Success postponed. Need for patience.

Seven of Wands　*Upright Meaning:* Sustained effort, negotiation, defending a position.

Reversed Meaning: Doubt, anxiety.

Eight of Wands　*Upright Meaning:* News, messages, travel, speed, hope.

Reversed Meaning: Miscommunication, delay.

Nine of Wands　*Upright Meaning:* Strength, self-protection, sacrifice. Also, the psychic wound.

Reversed Meaning: Obstacles, demands.

Ten of Wands　*Upright Meaning:* Overwhelm, work. Carrying a burden.

Reversed Meaning: As above, but habitually so.

Page of Wands　*Upright Meaning:* Good news, motivation, beginnings. As a person, a child or youth who is talkative and creative; an actor, writer, artist.

Reversed Meaning: Delay, communication problems.

Knight of Wands　*Upright Meaning:* Action. Whirlwind romance. Travel, moving house. As a person, an expressive, energetic individual.

Reversed Meaning: Delays and miscommunication. Insincerity.

Queen of Wands　*Upright Meaning:* Confidence, self-empowerment, creativity communication. As a person, a creative, inspirational woman.

Reversed Meaning: Interference, disruption.

King of Wands　*Upright Meaning:* Motivation and power. As a person, a dynamic, free spirit who doesn't judge.

Reversed Meaning: Restriction; the need to follow intuition.

APPENDIX III:
FURTHER READING

The Encyclopedia of Tarot, Volume I, Stuart R. Kaplan (US Games Systems Inc., 2001)

Fortune-Telling by Cards, Professor P. R. S. Foli (C. Arthur Pearson Ltd., 1915)

The Golden Dawn: An Account of the Teachings, Rites and Ceremonies of the Order of the Golden Dawn, Israel Regardie (Llewellyn, 1982; first published 1937–1940)

Initiation Into the Tarot: A Powerful System for Personal Spiritual Awakening, Naomi Ozaniec (Watkins, 2002)

The Pictorial Key to the Tarot, A. E. Waite (Dover Publications, 2005; first published by Rider, 1911)

Rachel Pollack's Tarot Wisdom: Spiritual Teachings and Deeper Meanings, Rachel Pollack (Llewellyn, 2016)

Ruth Ann Amberstone and Wald Amberstone (The Tarot School) online birth card calculator: https://tarotschool.com/Calculator.html

Tarot Mysteries: Rediscovering the Real Meaning of the Cards, Jonathan Dee (Zambezi Publishing, 2003)

The Ultimate Guide to Divination, Liz Dean (Fair Winds Press, 2017)

The Ultimate Guide to Tarot: A Beginner's Guide to the Cards, Spreads, and Revealing the Mystery of the Tarot, Liz Dean (Fair Winds Press, 2015)

The Visconti–Sforza Tarot Cards, Michael Dummett (George Braziller Inc., 1986)

ACKNOWLEDGMENTS

With thanks to Michael W. Young,
my agent Chelsey Fox, publisher Erik
Gilg, editors Jill Alexander, Tiffany Hill,
Meredith Quinn, and the great team at
Fair Winds. Gratitude to Ruth Ann and
Wald Amberstone of the Tarot School,
New York, and to those who attended my
first Soul Purpose workshop from
which the tarotscope, and later the idea
for this book, evolved: Linda, Yvonne,
Christina, Joanne, Laura, Emma, Fran,
Sarah, and Donna.

INDEX